Mom Loves Me Best

Mom Loves Me Best

(AND OTHER LIES YOU TOLD YOUR SISTER)

LINDA SUNSHINE

**Andrews McMeel
Publishing**

Kansas City

The author gratefully acknowledges the following:
Written with Michaela Weissman, the essay entitled
"Why Your Sister's Grass Is Always Greener" originally
appeared in a different format as "Wishful Thinkers" in the
February 1989 issue of *Special Reports*, copyright © 1989
by Whittle Communications. Reprinted with permission.
And many thanks to Michaela!

06 07 08 09 10 MLT 10 9 8 7 6 5 4 3 2 1

ISBN-13: 978-0-7407-5813-3
ISBN-10: 0-7407-5813-6

Library of Congress Control Number: 2005933697

www.andrewsmcmeel.com

Book design by Desiree Mueller

I dedicate this book to my darling
sister, Susan, with love . . . and to
the dear friends and family in my
life who are my adopted sisters:
Lena Tabori, Marsha Heckman,
Ella Stewart, Stephie Sunshine,
Alexis Dorenter, Lori Dorenter,
Diba Zweibach, Natasha Gordon,
and Katrina Fried.

Contents

Introduction

Meet My Sister, Susan

**The Flanders Sisters . . .
were like Night and Day.
Actually, they were more like
2 o'clock and 4 o'clock.**

Roz Chast,
Parallel Universes

I am writing this book for my sister, Susan, whom I love dearly, even though I told her to drop dead often enough when we were kids.

I was eighteen months old when Susan was born, and to be truthful, I don't think I've ever quite forgiven her for upstaging my solo act.

As kids, we shared a bedroom and, afraid of the dark, invented games to ward off sleep. One game, which we played every single night, was called "I'm sleeping." When one of us was too tired to talk anymore, she would call out, "I'm sleeping." The other would reply, "I'm sleeping." Then, in unison, we'd both sing out, "We're all sleeping." Okay, so it wasn't the most intellectually stimulating game (and the rules were way easy to learn) but it does point out one of the best features of having a sister: She makes you feel less alone.

It seems as though Susan and I were always together as young children. I remember the hours we spent, side by side, with our coloring books and 144 Crayolas. While we both loved to color, we had alarmingly different techniques.

I had a particular method that involved shading a border inside the black lines in a color just slightly darker than the filler space. I considered this very artistic.

My sister, ever more patient, was a total perfectionist (she still is!) and, thus, more meticulous about her coloring technique. It was always something of a crisis when she would go out of the lines. Usually, if this happened (say, when I, *by accident*, knocked her arm while she colored a delicate curve), she would throw down the book and refuse to finish the picture. "It's ruined," she would wail. "Why bother?" Sometimes she would cry.

So then we would get out the comics. Romance comics were our absolute favorites. We liked to read them out loud, and we fought over who got to be the beautiful girl and who got stuck with the boy parts. If she was still crying about the coloring book fiasco, I would agree to do the boy parts on the one condition that I could also do the sound effects. For instance, when the beautiful but stubborn heroine invariably tossed her engagement ring into the river, the lake, the ocean, the pond, or any other available body of water (a regular plot twist), someone would be obliged to read: "Kerrrr Plunk!" This was my all-time best sound effect, one which I can re-create today, upon request.

One Christmas, we got a portable tape recorder for a present, and I'm embarrassed to admit, we liked recording our rendition of a romance comic (sound effects and all), perhaps one of the world's first audiobooks on tape. Then we played it back and my brilliant "Kerrr Plunk!" would make us laugh until we fell off the bed.

Reading was always a favorite pastime for us, and eventually comics were replaced by books. Our taste in books was nothing to brag about, not that it was our fault. We were pretty much on our own in selecting books to read from the local bookmobile. Mom was a knitter, not a reader, and my dad, who'd married late in life, did not understand the concept of children's books. He tended to recommend biographies of his favorite political figures, a topic that did not spark my imagination but, as I was anxious to please him, dictated much of my reading. My book choices came as quite a surprise to my grade school teachers when I would give book reports about Harry S. Truman or Adlai Stevenson.

Left to our own devices, Susan and I went from Honey Bunch and Nancy Drew straight to *Peyton Place*, *Valley of the Dolls*, and *Gone with the Wind*. We loved Sidney Sheldon. In place of *Little Women* we read *Marjorie Morningstar*. And always, one of us wanted to read the exact book that the other had just started. I remember one vicious fight over *Sybil*, a book about a tortured woman with multiple personalities that so intrigued both of us that I went out and bought a duplicate copy while Susan was still reading hers.

I read faster than she did, and I liked to tell her the ending of the books before she could finish. Snapping the book closed, I declared, "Sybil dies in the end." The angrier this made her, the more I was pleased.

So I'd say, "I'm only kidding," and leave her to wonder whether I was lying when I told her Sybil died, or whether I was lying when I told her I was kidding. This was my way of keeping my sister on her toes and getting revenge for her not relinquishing the book when I wanted it.

When I was in fourth grade and Susan was a baby third-grader, we moved from our apartment into a house in the New Jersey suburbs. Our lives changed dramatically. We got our own bedrooms and learned about territorial imperatives.

And so, the "I'm sleeping" game was put to sleep and the real fighting began. I was older, wiser, and more mature than Susan and, almost always, instigated the fights. Susan only wanted to make nice, I only wanted my own way. I deeply resented having to always take care of my little sister when my parents went out for the evening, and to get back at Mom, I took it out on poor Susan.

My favorite torture was to drag her across the floor of our finished basement—by her hair. She hated this a lot. Even more, she hated when I would hide in some dark closet of the house and not come out until she was so scared by the thought of being left alone that she would start to cry.

I thought she deserved such treatment because she was so irritatingly perfect all the time.

There was lots of stuff about her that annoyed me. To impress my dad, I got good grades in elementary school and, after making honor roll in the seventh grade, was forever labeled the Brains of the family, a role I came to sorely regret. Susan was the Pretty One and, for this, I wanted to strangle her. Can you blame me? Given the choice, what preadolescent girl wants to be smart instead of pretty? Let's see: Lindsay Lohan or the foreign exchange student who wins the National Spelling Bee?

Susan did everything the way girls were supposed to, as if she were a character from a romance comic. She joined after-school clubs, learned to twirl a baton, and went out with nice Jewish boys. I hung out with the Italian guys, smoked cigarettes, and wore heavy black eyeliner. Throughout high school, we traveled in totally different circles and tried to avoid bumping into each other as much as possible.

I went to college in Ithaca, New York, and she went to Washington, D.C. We would speak on the phone but I remember visiting her only once while we were in college. When Susan graduated, a year after I did, she moved into my apartment in New York City where I had been living since my graduation. I was completely absorbed in building a career in publishing. Susan had a job selling airtime for NBC, which did not much interest her. She lived with me for a year, trying to decide whether or not to marry her college boyfriend. One night after our favorite evening of watching *Mary Tyler Moore* and pigging out on ice cream, Oreos, and M&M's, we started talking about our childhood. "You know," she said, "I always envied the way you talked back to your teachers."

I never imagined that my sister envied anything about me. "You envied me for that?" I marveled, "I envied the way you looked in a bikini."

For most of the evening—and well into the early morning—we revealed the things we'd always envied or admired about each other. The list seemed endless.

While we'd been sisters all our lives, it wasn't until that night that we became friends. She forgave me for beating her up all the time and I forgave her for her straight hair that never needed ironing.

We still fight now and then. Of course, I no longer drag her across the floor by her hair or try to scare her to tears, although sometimes we say things to each other that are not very nice. But we always forgive each other. If, as they say in the movies, love means never having to say you are sorry, then I think that loving your sister means never having to apologize for being a complete bitch every now and then.

Despite the cracks I make about my sister in this book and the way I treated her as a child, I know that I got really lucky in the sibling department.

Here's a deep dark sister-secret that we've never shared with anyone, other than our respective shrinks, of course. Once, in the heat of a ferocious adolescent fight, as she defended herself by raising her hand, I kicked my sister so hard that I broke her little finger. (It was an accident; I was trying to break her skull.) Yet, instead of ratting me out, she told Mom that she'd walked into a door and her label changed from the Pretty One to the Klutz. Still she never squealed.

How could you *not* love a sister like that?

Take This Test:

Are You a Good Sister, or What?

"You got your father's looks. The both of you," Mom says to me and my sister when she gets in that one talking mood about her mistakes in life. And she tells me I had better get busy working on my charm. "Well, be grateful you don't have a weight problem," she says, then looks straight at my sister.

Lynda Barry,
Come Over, Come Over

We begin this book with a pop quiz, just like your worst days in high school. The reason for the test is simple: Because you have known your sister for a very long time, it is often difficult to see her as she truly exists in real life. Women sometimes have romantic, unrealistic notions about their sisters. You still see your sibling as a child. Psychiatrists call this Frozen Misconceptions (a real term that I didn't make up but wish that I had). It is sometimes a shock to realize that your sister is an adult, with a life of her own, and that she no longer depends on you to tell her what she thinks. (Although she could probably still use your advice about her makeup.)

At almost any age, it is difficult, if not impossible, to avoid conflict with your sister. Many things about her may drive you up a wall, especially because she represents so much of what you can't stand about yourself.

The following test will be helpful in allowing you to focus on the areas of conflict you may have with your sister. Try to answer as openly and honestly as possible. Do not look up the scores at the end of the quiz before completing each and every question. And keep your eyes to yourself!

1. Overall, how do you rate your relationship with your sister?

    a. Good
    b. Passable
    c. An act of self-sacrifice

2. What about your sister threatens you most?

    a. Her acomplishments
    b. Her husband/boyfriend/life partner
    c. Her inner thighs

3. How would you define your relationship with your sister?

    a. Equal
    b. One of you is the leader, the other follows
    c. She gets all the good stuff

4. Expressing emotion is:

    a. Easy for her, hard for me
    b. Easy for me, hard for her
    c. Not considered polite in our family

5. Do you encourage your sister's involvement in new interests or activities?

    a. Yes
    b. No
    c. Only if there's something in it for me

6. If you answered "a" or "c" to the above, what method do you employ to encourage your sister in new activities?

    a. Talk to her

    b. Get involved with her

    c. Kick, scream and bite until she does what you tell her to do

7. How often do you compare yourself with your sister?

    a. Hardly ever

    b. Occasionally

    c. Whenever Mom calls

8. What activities do you enjoy doing with your sister?

    a. Exercising

    b. Shopping

    c. Borrowing money

9. Are you influenced by your sister's opinion?

    a. Yes

    b. No

    c. Only when she agrees with me

10. In what areas do you compete with your sister?

    a. In our social lives

    b. In our professional lives

    c. In our mother's kitchen

11. How often do you see your sister?

    a. At least once a week

    b. At every major holiday/family dinner

    c. At every family funeral

12. How often do you fight with your sister?
    a. Hardly ever
    b. All the time
    c. Only when she's a bitch

13. When do you seek your sister's advice?
    a. Hardly ever
    b. All the time
    c. Whenever your therapist permits

14. How do you deal with a point of conflict with your sister?
    a. Confront it
    b. Ignore it
    c. Kick, bite, and scream

15. Which of you is more likely to compromise or apologize?
    a. Your sister
    b. You
    c. None of the above

16. What would happen if you ever shared your true feelings with your sister?
    a. She'd cry
    b. You'd feel closer to each other
    c. Someone would wind up in a cast

17. What is the most positive aspect of your relationship with your sister?
    a. Companionship
    b. Shared family history
    c. Her vacation house

18. If your sister had only one week to live,
    what would you want to tell her?

    a. You love her
    b. You'll take care of Mom
    c. You lied about her being adopted

19. The things you like best about your sister:

    a. Her personality
    b. Her sense of humor
    c. Her shoes

20. The things your sister likes best about you:

    a. Your honesty
    b. Your compassion
    c. Your car

Score: If you answered "a" to the majority of these questions you are a Big Liar, Liar, Pants on Fire, Young Lady! Go to your room and while you are there, clean out that closet of yours!

If you answered "b" to most of these questions, then you are semi–well adjusted and seem to have a decent relationship with your sister. Overall, you are a good, if boring, sibling.

If you answered "c" to most of the questions in this test you get a gold star for honesty but a black mark for being so obnoxious. You would do well to apologize to your sister for being such a pain in the neck, and, while you are at it, return the jewelry you borrowed from her.

History, Sociology, and Other Background Stuff

> **Every now and then we think about my sisters and hope they're doing well but we don't dwell upon the matter, as that only allows the kidnappers to win.**

"Chipped Beef,"
David Sedaris, *Naked*

Dear Linda,

My sister, Adele, was adopted into our family when she was a baby. Recently, she found her birth family and has been spending a great deal of time with them. My parents and I are beginning to suspect that she likes them more than she likes us.

Personally, I would really hate to see her go live with them. She has several pairs of shoes and a half dozen sweaters that I like to borrow from time to time. If she goes, my wardrobe would be greatly depleted and my mom would be upset.

How can we trick her into liking us better so that she won't be tempted to leave?

Sylvia

Dear Sylvia,

My advice is to let her go live with her birth family. In no time at all, she will find them just as irritating and annoying as her adopted family and you will get her back.

Linda

In the Beginning

In the beginning was your mother. And She spoke the words. And the words were these: "Sisters who love each other do not fight."

And the mother's words were, well, wrong. (Sorry, Mom!)

The truth is this: Sisters who love each other fight all the time.

If you don't understand how a woman could both love her sister dearly and want to wring her neck at the same time, then you were probably an only child.

Ancient History

Great sister acts have appeared throughout recorded history, dating all the way back to ancient Greek mythology when, on Mount Olympus, there were two lovely bands of sisters, the Muses and the Graces. In her book *Mythology*, renowned scholar Edith Hamilton writes extensively about the Muses and the Graces, and I was going to research the subject but Ms. Hamilton's book was checked out of the library on the day I had the idea. (Good for Ms. Hamilton!)

Anyway, if I start all the way back in Ancient Greece, it will take forever and a day to get to the Simpson girls (Jessica and Ashlee), so let's just flash forward several thousand years to the 2000s, a decade to which I can relate.

Modern Trends in Sibling Relationships, Seriously

Several of today's societal and sociological trends have affected sibling relationships. Among these are family size, average life span, women in the workforce, family mobility, and divorce rates. I know that these trends are accurate because each and every one has been discussed by Dr. Phil and Oprah.

Family Size

Since the dawn of time and last Tuesday night, we first notice that family size has shrunk significantly. Mom and Dad probably came from much larger families than the one they created with you. Your parents may have each had three or four siblings. And your grandparents probably came from even larger families. A hundred years ago, families with a dozen or more kids were not at all uncommon. That all changed when the cost of Nikes jumped to more than $100 a pair.

Few people in our society today can afford to support more than two kids, and thank heavens for that. Can you imagine sharing a bathroom with eleven other sisters? It would be midnight before you got to shower.

Average Life Span

Our families are not only smaller, but each of us tends to live longer. In 1900, the average American lived to the age of forty-seven; today, many people don't even start looking to adopt a Chinese baby until they hit fifty.

Now, our average life span for men is seventy-four, and most women live well into their eighties. This means that life with your sister can last anywhere from sixty to eighty years! Remember that your sister may be the only person on the planet who will see you make the transition from high chair to wheelchair.

Working Mamas

Over the past few decades, the increased number of working mothers has also had a tremendous effect on sibling relationships as well as the popularity of working-mom magazines designed to sell $900 baby strollers and alleviate the guilt of leaving the care of your children to a Guatemalan woman.

It is generally acknowledged that when not monitored by a PCA (Personally Committed Adult) children tend to spend more time with their hands in the cookie jar and their fingers on the X-rated DVDs.

Even our media role models have changed. Concerned and caring moms on TV who we grew to love and admire like Patricia Heaton on *Everyone Loves Raymond* have been replaced with those scary desperate housewives.

Family Mobility

Working moms and dads travel more than ever these days, resulting in Increased Family Mobility and the likelihood that Mom or Dad will get offered a new job somewhere across the country and insist that you and your siblings move with them to some god-forsaken city where your cell phone gets lousy reception.

Changing schools and friends is hard on kids and can often make them depressed and lonely enough to form closer ties with a sister. Children caught in this predicament should be advised not to panic. Parents need to remind them that, eventually, they will meet other kids in school who will relieve them of the burden of being nice to their siblings.

Divorce, Mommy Dating, and Remarriage

Divorce rates, single-parent families, and remarriages have changed the way that families develop and relate to each other. Younger children may have a difficult time adjusting when parents divorce and remarry, especially when new children from previous marriages are brought into the family. These stepsiblings or stepsibs, as they are called, have created a whole new genre in the family structure. Stepsibs are somewhat less important than your youngest sibling and rank just above the family dog in the birth order factor.

For older children, divorce can be doubly traumatic after Dad moves out and Mom starts dating again, especially if Mom has more dates than her teenage daughters and/or happens to date Ashton Kutcher. Can you imagine competing with that?

Psychological Factors: Stress and Anxiety

Sociologists have noted that the twin components of life in the 2000s are stress and anxiety. Previously, it was thought that just because no one talked about anxiety until the latter part of the 1970s, it did not exist.

Recent discoveries, however, point out that anxiety has been around for more than two hundred years and was first mentioned by George Washington as early as 1760 when he wrote in his diary about meeting a plump but plucky widow named Martha who, Washington noted, "makes me as anxious as a cat in a room full of rocking chairs."

Stress, of course, first entered the American vernacular in 1969 when Richard Nixon was elected president.

You're Only Jung Once

Carl Jung, a shrink who became almost as famous as Sigmund Freud (but not quite) used the word "persona" to describe the mask that we all hide behind. Some of us create better masks than others. For instance, give Brad Pitt and George Clooney an A+ and Michael Jackson a big fat F.

Jung claimed that everyone, not just cute actors and misguided pop stars, has a publicly presented self. At an early age, children develop a "persona" that is acceptable to the authority figures in his or her life. Kids can often be very effective at putting on a show for their parents. Mom and Dad may think you are a little angel and never even suspect you are stealing loose bills from Mom's purse whenever she's not looking.

Your sister, on the other hand, *knows everything*!

While you can hide your true self from Mom and Dad, your sister knows the very core of you. She sees you being mean to the family cat; she hears you lie to your best friend; she knows when you've cheated on your chemistry test. More than Santa Claus, your sister knows when you've been bad or good. And she is not averse to using this information when it suits her, for instance, when she wants to borrow your very favorite cashmere sweater set. (Blackmail was quite possibly invented by somebody's sister.)

With this kind of leverage, is it any wonder that sibling relationships are fraught with conflict?

Uncommon Bonds

In all likelihood, there have been times when you expressed your desire that your sister shrivel up and disappear off the face of the earth.

Parents often mistake such statements as proof of real tension between sisters. They believe that sisters who yell and scream at each other may be expressing real animosity.

Wrong. It is an absolute given that sisters love each other. How could it be otherwise? Your sister is the only creature on the planet who shares your heritage, history, environment, DNA, bone structure, and contempt for stupid Aunt Gertie.

Your sister is like your own heartbeat—she's a part of you that's easy to take for granted.

There are many special moments between sisters when they act loving and generous toward each other but, usually, not within sight of anyone else. Say, when your sister suggests that you've lost weight (when you both know that is an outright lie) or she loans you money at a very low interest rate or that time she sat up all night holding your hand because Rocky Rissoto didn't ask you to your senior prom. But parents rarely see those times.

More often, sisters are at each other's throats around their parents. Given the nature of this phenomena, parents have often marveled that it's something of a miracle their children make it to adulthood without killing each other or, at the very least, poking out an eye.

Chronological Chart
Stages of Sibling Relationships

In the following chart, we show the five basic stages in the development of a typical sibling relationship.

1. Pre-Birth. Encompasses the period before the arrival of a sibling. During this time, Mom carefully prepares you for the coming event by constantly talking about how you are about to get a new friend for life. She predicts that family life is about to change radically but as far as you (the child) are concerned, all that really happens is that Mommy gets really, really fat.

2. Post-Birth. Mom disappears for a few days, although to you (the child), this feels like five years. Daddy tells you how happy everyone is but your main concern is Who will cook dinner tonight? When Dad treats you to McDonald's every night, you tend to forget about Mom all together. When Mom does finally return, you are likely to ask, "Uh, Mom who?" Then you notice she is carrying a tiny bundle, your sister. As far as you can tell, this prune-faced, soft headed, not-yet-a-person does nothing but spit up and howl all night. Why are people drooling over her? You have stuffed animals who are way cuter.

3. Early Childhood. A relatively uneventful period—just before your sister begins walking and talking and borrowing your stuff—when you live with the grand illusion that your relationship with your sister will never change. She's not so bad, you think. Sometimes she can even be entertaining, sort of like a talking doll that does not need batteries.

4. Mid-Childhood Crisis. The arguments begin. You fight about property, clothes, friends, personal rights, school, and the world in general, but still you see your childhood as unending and unchanging. This is, of course, way before your first menstrual cramp, when you still think it's pretty cool to be a girl.

5. Adolescence. Everything changes. Everything! Your body, sense of humor (if you have one), your taste in music, clothes, books, and boys. Your hair and fingernails undergo massive transformations. You may get inked or pierced in places you didn't even know existed during childhood. You can no longer play with or even talk to your sister. This causes a great deal of friction in the family as everyone fights for control. Since no one can ever win such a battle, your emotional barometer now has only two settings: arctic ice and nuclear meltdown.

6. Adulthood. You leave the house and move on with your life—get an education or a job, move in with someone, marry, work, have kids, whatever. You recall your childhood as golden. You are trapped with those previously mentioned Frozen Misconceptions. Until you go into serious therapy, you only remember the idyllic times of early childhood.

7. Senior Sisters. You wake up one morning and discover you have gray hairs in places that used to be hairless. How did this happen? Suddenly you are spending far too much time talking about mortgages, cholesterol, television shows, dead people, and retirement communities. You realize, for certain, you will never hitchhike cross-country, sing in a rock band, wear a size 6, be an astronaut, meet Oprah, read a menu in a dark restaurant (even with glasses), swim naked, run for president, stay up all night for any reason whatsoever, dance on Broadway, be a writer/director/producer, function without a tweezer, or eat gummy bears and a chili dog at the same time.

These different stages can best be understood by the kind of language one uses during these phases, as exemplified in the following list:

1. Pre-Birth

> "Why can't I have a baby sister?"
>
> "Why? Why? Why? Why?"

2. Post-Birth

> "Do we have to keep her?"
>
> "No fair!"

3. Early Childhood

> "Let's play patty-cake."
>
> "Here is how to use the remote."
>
> "Can I have some of your Twinkie?"

4. Mid-Childhood Crisis

> "I'm Mommy's favorite!"
>
> "You weren't even alive then."
>
> "You were an accident."
>
> "There's no Santa Claus."
>
> "I'm telling!"
>
> "Do over."
>
> "Stop repeating me."
>
> "STOP REPEATING ME!!!!"

5. Adolescence

"Your best friend is fat."

"You're fat."

"I'm telling."

"Get out of my closet."

"This is MINE!"

"You let her get away with murder."

"You *always* take her side."

"It's not *fair*."

6. Adulthood

"You're majoring in WHAT?"

"Your boyfriend is an idiot."

"Looks more like a half carat to me."

"Of course I'll be your maid of honor."

"Why can't I have a baby niece?"

7. Senior Sister

"I never smoked pot."

"I am just *considering* BOTOX."

"The Republicans aren't as bad as I thought."

"What was all the fuss about?"

"My first marriage didn't count."

"Does this come in an extra large?"

Infancy:

Baby Sisters Are Like Goats

A baby sister is nicer than a goat.
You'll get used to her.

Lynn Alpern and Esther Blumenfeld,
Oh, Lord, I Sound Just Like Mama

Smile and the world smiles with you.
Cry and you go to your room.

My mom

Dear Linda,

My older sister thinks she is right about everything. She constantly voices her opinion about my kids, my job, my decorating style, my hair, my clothes, and how I play Scrabble. She even criticizes the way I park my car. She thinks she knows everything. This causes great conflict between us. What can I do?

Sarah from Saratoga

Dear Sarah from Saratoga,

Being an older sister myself, I can sympathize with your situation and understand the difficulty in your relationship.

So I will share with you the same advice I give to my own little sister: Open up your mind and your heart and accept that your older sister knows, better than you, what is right for you and you should do everything she suggests.

If you follow this advice, I think your relationship will greatly improve.

Linda

The Birth Order Principle

In the late 1980s, experts in the field of sibling psychosis determined that where you were born in the family structure was critical to your development. Your B.O. (that's Birth Order) determined whether you turned out to be Mom's Beloved Can-Do-No-Wrong Child or the Cry-Baby Kid. In childhood, you either get to shop for a new bike with Daddy or you have to play checkers with only nine pieces and a button. As a sister, you will soon learn that life isn't always fair and that nobody gets all the Mallomars for herself.

Understanding your position, then, in the family constellation can be extremely helpful in determining your odds of either getting a new Ford Explorer for your eighteenth birthday or a roll of Scotch tape.

There are three basic positions in the Birth Order Principle: Eldest, Middle, and Baby. With each additional child, the cycle repeats itself because Mom and Dad are too tired, by then, to invent new methods of child rearing and they simply recycle old habits.

Each position in the family structure has its relative advantages and its drawbacks. A brief explanation follows.

The Eldest

For as long as you were an Only Child, life was bliss. You had everything you could possibly want for happiness—only you did not know it. You assumed this was the way life worked. Like Adam and Eve in the Garden, you learned—too late—that ignorance is not only bliss, it is way better than having to share everything you hold sacred.

If a sibling did not appear before you learned to talk, your first sentence was probably, "Why can't I have a baby sister?" All your friends have siblings and their houses always seem to have a lot more toys and different kinds of cookies than your house.

Be Careful What You Ask For

Asking for a sibling was the first major mistake of your young life. All that Only Child attention made you overly generous and heady with power.

Before the new baby arrives, Mom assures you that nothing will detract from her time with you. This is a whopping big lie, as you soon discover. Once baby sister comes into the house, Mommy will never have time to sing you "Itsy Bitsy Spider" and Daddy will be too tired to play horsey like he used to. You will soon discover that you are the only rational person in the house who does not go bananas just because your raisin-faced sister can burp like your cousin Lenny after he drinks a Mountain Dew.

Fairly soon after her arrival, you will acknowledge that you've made a horrible mistake and that bringing this creature into your private domain was not such a good idea. "Take her back!" you demand. "I changed my mind."

You are utterly amazed when your parents insist on keeping her. If Mommy returns a skirt because she thinks it makes her look fat and she refuses to get you a puppy because of the poop that has to be cleaned up, you wonder why she wants to keep that screaming, dirty-diaper-making thing in the house. This is when you will first grasp the meaning of "nonreturnable," a dreadful term that will haunt you later in life, especially in expensive shoe stores.

It will take some time, several years in fact, but eventually, you will come around to seeing that there are certain advantages to having the little snot-nose around, particularly when it is raining outside.

Advantages of Having a Baby Sister

1. Your baby sister will always let you select the board game, especially after you threaten to lock her in the basement and turn out the lights.

2. You can usually con her into selling you Boardwalk, dirt cheap.

3. She will let you make up card games with elaborate rules that you can change if she starts to win. ("Wait a minute! I forget to mention that tens are wild!")

4. She will help you color in the really big spaces.

5. You will always have someone to blame for the mud tracks on the kitchen floor, the mess in the sink, the unset table, or the spinach on the ceiling.

6. You can do mean things to her and she won't tell your parents.

7. She lets you borrow her stuff.

8. She asks *you* questions instead of Mom, making you feel smug and confident in the rightness of your own opinions (a trait that might not serve too well in later life, unless you decide to go into politics or teaching).

9. She takes out the garbage when it is your turn, in exchange for a promise not to abandon her when Mom and Dad go out at night.

10. She thinks you are worldly and cool. (She may be the only one!)

11. After awhile, you come to appreciate the ways in which your baby sister worships you and you begin to admire her good sense. You also begin to recapture some of the sense of power you felt as an Only Child. Unfortunately, your sister will outgrow her heroine worship at about the age of seven and a half, leaving you to conclude that baby sisters are okay as long as they remain young, innocent, gullible, and bad card players.

The Baby

As the baby, you do not know what life was like *without* your sister. She has been around since your own personal Day One on Planet Earth and is as much a part of your world as the mobile hanging over your crib.

Advantages of Being the Youngest Sister

1. You are the cutest.

2. Your older sister makes you feel more secure. When Mommy and Daddy argue, she holds your hand and tells you not to worry. She protects you because she is braver than you.

3. You often feel like it is you and your sister against the world.

4. You always have someone close by who is tall enough to reach the Ding Dongs in the upper cabinets.

5. You fantasize that when you are older, your sister will introduce you to cute boys. (You are in for a rude awakening but never mind.)

6. Your sister is always there to teach you how to use a Kotex, how to break the Parental Control code on the TiVo, and to explain the meaning of "French kiss" and "going all the way." (Inevitably your sister's information will be totally wrong but you will not discover this until you are twenty-seven years old.)

Disadvantages of Being the Youngest Sister

1. You will always be younger than your sister, and even when you are both grandmothers, she will think she knows more than you.

2. Your sister's problems will seem much more important to your parents than yours.

3. Your sister will often do things to scare you.

4. You will often be called bad names by your sister who will learn how to curse long before you do.

5. You will get stuck with hand-me-downs and your sister will never let you forget it.

6. Despite all this, the real danger of being the youngest is that you lose whatever status you have in the event that another sibling enters the house. The fall from grace from being the "youngest" to the "middle" can cause a severe case of the bends.

Pity the Poor Middle Child

Have sympathy for the middle child for her lot in life is not easy. The Middle exists in a kind of vacuum. She does not get the pressure to perform like the Eldest or the attention of the Baby. Basically, she is left to her own devices and will spend most of her childhood grabbing at straws. While this is painful in childhood, it does allow for a certain amount of freedom and independence in adolescence and adulthood. The Middle is pretty much free to do her own thing, mostly because no one is really paying much attention.

The Plight of the Middle

1. She will often rebel to attract attention and she will always be the last one to arrive at the dinner table.

2. She will believe in outrageous haircuts and clothes made of rubber or leather.

3. She will endure multiple piercings and getting inked on some very sensitive body parts.

4. She will sneak out of the house at night to meet her boyfriend, and no one in the family will notice she is gone.

5. She would die before wearing a hand-me-down.

6. She will often attend college on another coast, using the distance for the reason why her parents never visit.

7. She will never have more than two children.

8. Her favorite cookies will be Oreos.

Dear Linda,

All I remember about my childhood was the constant fighting. I know we all loved each other but, still, what a racket we made! It went on all day and night. Growing up in my house was like living in Beirut. Can you explain this to me?

Arleen

Dear Arleen,

There's a good reason why there was so much yelling going on in your childhood. Psychologists call this the Trickle-Down Theory of Family Aggression.

According to the principles of this theory:

Daddy yells at Mommy. Mommy yells at the Eldest. Eldest pulls Middle's hair. Middle pokes the Baby. Baby kicks the dog. Dog pees on the carpet. Mommy yells at dog. Daddy yells at Mommy. (Repeat ad infinitum.)

Cheers!
Linda

All I Really Need to Know I Learned from My Sister

My sister taught me everything I really need to know, and she was only in the sixth grade at the time.

Her credo weathered the test of adolescence and served me well as an adult. She was so right on, in fact, that I never had to waste time inventing my own credo—I simply copied hers.

Here are the lessons I learned from my sister.

1. Share everything with your sister but don't expect anything in return.

2. Play by my rules. They're fair, I promise.

3. Don't hit me or I'll tell.

4. Touch my things and you die.

5. Clean up after yourself and me.

6. Lend me money when I ask.

7. Buy me expensive birthday gifts and write sappy cards to go with them.

8. Leave the house when I bring home a cool friend.

9. Goldfish and hamsters and grandparents all die some day. So will you. I am living forever.

10. When you go out into the world, remember to bring me back a Diet Coke.

Middle Childhood:

Take a Picture!

Should you be a teenager blessed with uncommon good looks, document this state of affairs by the taking of photographs. It is the only way anyone will ever believe you in years to come.

Fran Lebowitz,
Social Studies

Dear Linda,

My sister's boyfriend wants to sleep with me. I think he also wants to have sex with my brother. I find that thought disgusting and yet oddly compelling. What should I do?

Maggie

Dear Maggie,

Let me know when I can watch your family work this out on _Jerry Springer_.

Linda

Sibling Rivalry

Sibling rivalry is one of the most basic, elemental aspects of having or being a sister. It is a required condition of your siblinghood and not an elective course like, say, home economics. You simply cannot be living in the same house, with the same parents and a finite number of toys and Cheez Doodles, without incurring at least a minimal amount of kicking, biting, and screaming.

While there are numerous case studies of sibling rivalry charted in almost every developmental age group from one day old to just-moments-before-death, scientists have recently discovered that the predisposition toward sibling rivalry begins even before birth. In a recent federally funded study, molecular biologists at the famed University of Kennebunkport were scrounging around in the DNA strand one afternoon when they happened upon an actual living gene that causes sibling rivalry. They aptly named this gene the Squabble Factor.

The Squabble Factor

For those less scientifically minded (who probably cut bio class every Tuesday to hang out in the girls' bathroom and smoke cigarettes), it should be explained that DNA is part of your genetic makeup and is every bit as important as your mascara, blusher, and tweezers. DNA is like a blueprint that determines the color of your eyes, the length of your legs, the shape of your earlobes, and the texture of your hair. If you are not particularly pleased with your looks (and who is?), you should blame your DNA instead of your hairdresser or the blueberry muffins you eat for breakfast every morning.

Simply put, every one of us possesses a gene predisposing us toward rivalry, competition, and fits of jealous rage with any past, present, or future sibling. (This includes stepsiblings who may appear later in life.)

The presence of the Squabble Factor is evidenced by many well-documented childhood symptoms. The gene causes young children to covet the front seat of all moving vehicles, hoard all the M&M's, borrow clothes without asking permission, and tell lies to babysitters and substitute teachers. It is the gene that enables young children to whine in an extremely high pitch. Examples of the Squabble Factor can be found in such phrases as: "If she can stay up until nine, why can't I?" and "Why does she always get to hold the remote?" as well as the ever popular "She makes me want to puke!"

The Squabble Factor enables children to develop their

cursing skills at a remarkably early age and to remember a string of invectives, even if heard only once, uttered by a parent when the car got a flat tire in the middle of a thunderstorm. It is also the gene that carries the basic tactics for hand-to-hand combat fighting, including such basics as hair pulling, spitball shooting, and under-the-table shin kicking.

Fairy Tales Can Come True

Sibling rivalry has a long history, dating back to the time of the Brothers Grimm. One of the first recorded cases of traumatic sibling rivalry was that of Cinderella S., the youngest, thinnest, and prettiest of several girls in her family. As a case study we are all aware of how Cinderella defied her mean stepmom and enacted revenge on her rotten stepsisters by winning the hand of the most handsome and richest prince in the kingdom. Her story has been used for centuries to demonstrate the obvious moral: It always pays to wear the right shoes.

Sibling rivalry is not without its benefits. What happens between sisters is that they squabble, make up, share the graham crackers, squabble over the last cookie, make up, share the potato chips, squabble over the last one, and so on. Then they sit down at the dinner table and throw spaghetti at each other. These tussles teach children how to live with others, cope with victories and defeats, and deal with their own nonloving feelings. Through their brothers and sisters, children learn how the world operates and they are better prepared themselves for their future lives as frustrated housewives or henpecked husbands.

They also become well suited for careers in education or fast-food service.

Three Little Rules for Winning the Sibling Wars

1. The first and most important rule is to always, always remember that acts of violence between siblings are absolutely forbidden when either parent is within earshot. Take your battles to the basement, the laundry room, the attic, the garage, the closet, or the walk-in fridge—anywhere where your parents will not see or hear you.

2. If caught with your hands around your sibling's neck, your foot on her back, or your fist posed over her head, deny, deny, deny that you are causing pain for the little brat. Claim you are in the middle of teaching your kid sister that latest hip-hop step or fall back on the "We're only horsing around" defense.

3. If caught without hope of escape, especially if a bloody nose or broken bones are involved, *do not* accept the responsibility. Plead your case with the Sibling Fifth Amendment: "She started it!" and hang tough. Even Dr. Phil would have to acknowledge that any child who cannot palm off responsibility to cover her ass is just not going to survive the 2000s.

Dear Linda,

My mother always wanted to be a journalist but she said she abandoned her career because of me and my brother. Mom's been writing poetry for thirty years. She has written tons of poems about my brother, such as one called "What Is a Son?" I've heard this poem so often I could quote it verbatim from the time I was ten years old.

What is he do you suppose?
Pockets bulging with rocks and toads
Dreaming of fishing while in church
Where will it end, this fugitive
    search?
Doctor, lawyer, Indian chief—
These thoughts bring me no grief—
For no matter what he becomes,
He will always be my son!

My brother did not turn out to be a doctor or a lawyer. He was always getting into trouble as a kid and currently he's doing time for passing bad checks, yet my mother goes on reciting "What Is a Son?" while we take a bus to visit him in jail. She still thinks he is going to grow up and become a cardiologist or the next Johnnie Cochran.

My mother has written poems about our rowboat, her canary, the washing machine, even about her marinara sauce, but she's never written one about me, her only daughter. When I ask her to write about me, she says, "I don't know what it is, Janey, but I just can't put pen to paper about you." What's the deal?

Janey

Dear Janey,

Clearly, you are the victim of rampant sibling favoritism. This is incurable, so I would give up on asking for a poem from your mom. Mom's priorities are so firmly in place that you should be thankful if she remembers your middle name.

If I were you, I'd move far away from home and stop visiting your brother in jail.

And keep in mind that the ways in which we become petty, jealous, and envious as adults can be traced directly to the ways our mothers treated us in comparison with our siblings. So hang tough and prepare for some difficult relationships with men in your future.

Linda

Favoritism

Nothing breeds sibling rivalry more than the dreaded disease of parental favoritism, one of the most prominent yet cleverly concealed ailments of family life.

Make no mistake. Favoritism is an insidious, difficult-to-diagnose disease that can go undetected for years. Parents are loath to admit that they favor one child over the other. "I love both my children exactly the same," parents will insist. As any sibling can tell you, this is a whopping big lie.

According to the latest statistics, the odds of any parent feeling equally about their children are about the same as Osama bin Laden winning the Nobel Peace Prize.

Children who grow up in an environment haunted by favoritism are at a loss to change the family dynamic that breeds such a disease. The victim, that is the child who is constantly short-changed, is unlikely to be believed when she accuses her parents of favoritism. Her cries of "You always let *her* get away with everything" are vehemently denied by that parent. The child is often punished for "being too sensitive" or "making mountains out of molehills," to use typical parental euphemisms. "It's not true," a parent will insist. "We treat you both exactly the same. Now shut up and go to your room. I have to work on your sister's term paper."

The favored child will often develop a sense of superiority, power, and entitlement. For obvious reasons, she will do nothing to alter these family dynamics, unless she is a complete pinhead.

In refusing to admit that one child is favored over the other, parents make this disease even more difficult to diagnose. While the varieties of favoritism are endless, there are several clear-cut signs that children are victims of this disease. Read the following list and check the items that apply to your childhood.

Checklist:
Telltale Signs of Favoritism

	The Favored Child	The Victim
Nickname	❑ "Darling"	❑ "Numbskull"
Lunchbox	❑ Barbie patent leather	❑ Brown bag
Lunch	❑ Sushi	❑ Leftover sushi
Bed room	❑ Master suite and private bath	❑ Basement
Transportation	❑ SUV	❑ Metro Card
Vacations	❑ East Hampton	❑ Backyard
Money Loan	❑ Doesn't have to pay back	❑ Pay back with 8 percent interest
Computer	❑ Power Mac G5 and 27" flat screen	❑ Electric typewriter
Curfew	❑ Before sunrise	❑ 9:00 sharp
College	❑ Anything Ivy League	❑ School of Hard Knocks
Clothing	❑ Prada	❑ Sears
Allowance	❑ American Express Platinum Card	❑ $7.00 a week
After School	❑ Ballet, piano, horseback riding	❑ Babysitting, paper route

The number of check marks in each column will tell you whether you are the favored child or a victim of favoritism, although the symptoms are so obvious that only an idiot would need to take a test to find out. But never mind, because truthfully there is little that can be done to alleviate favoritism. Like the common cold, there is no cure, although there are certain illegal drugs that can temporarily lessen the pain.

There is only one remedy to favoritism: Be an only child.

Sibling Solidarity

Occasionally, siblings can and do form an allegiance, which is known as Sibling Solidarity. Usually, this happens when children share a mutual bond or have survived a trauma together. Say, for example, when the cable TV goes on the blink and there is nothing to watch for a whole evening except reruns of *Friends*. Children can and do survive such catastrophes, and often this kind of shared panic can draw siblings closer together for periods as long as twenty-four hours. In one such recorded case, two teenage sisters in Tacoma, Washington, remained civil to each other for an entire weekend when a freak thunderstorm brought down the satellite dish and, for four days, disrupted all television service. (And the DVD player didn't work either!) Though the kids weathered the trauma with apparent ease, their parents, Millie and Franco, had to be hospitalized for posttraumatic stress disorder. Both of them are still on twice-daily doses of Zoloft.

As this family discovered, though it is difficult for parents to live with kids who fight all the time, united siblings can pose an even greater threat to their stability and sanity. This is why parents are often advised to never have more children than television sets in any household.

Sibling Secrets

Sibling Solidarity can also occur when children form a pact against their parents. This pact may involve sharing a secret, such as

- "We stayed up till midnight when Mom and Dad played bridge at the Conners'."
- "We saw Mommy dent the SUV in the parking lot at Target!"
- "We lied about finishing our homework."
- "We saw Daddy kissing Mrs. Conners in the laundry room."
- "We killed the cleaning lady and buried her in the backyard."

Sibling Loyalty

Prolonged Sibling Solidarity can sometimes lead to Sibling Loyalty. Take the following test and check off all items that apply to you and your sister. Then have your sister take the test and see how she scores. You may discover that your sister is more loyal than you thought. Or you may learn that she cannot be trusted with your kids, your best china, or your social security number—especially your social security number.

❏ We do not abandon each other in the middle of shopping malls, crosswalks, or complicated jigsaw puzzles.

❏ We resolve our conflicts without spilling blood or breaking bones, if possible.

❏ We occasionally compliment each other.

❏ We help each other with homework and do not give false answers that would prove humiliating in the classroom.

❏ We do not draw mustaches or black out teeth on photographs of our siblings.

❏ We do not air our differences in front of company at the dinner table.

❏ We make nice and give kisses to relatives from out of town, even the really gross ones.

❏ We share our clothes without charging exorbitant rates for dry cleaning.

❏ We do not react to our sibling's date by sticking a finger in our mouth and pretending to barf. We especially do not do this on her wedding day.

❏ We protect each other when a guy in the street yells out a rude comment or when an irate ex-spouse threatens to drive his truck through the living room.

❏ We cooperate as best we can, except when sharing a kitchen and making a meal together.

❏ We do not reveal each other's secrets to friends and/or prospective dates (unless such secrets would make us more interesting to others).

Sibling Contamination

During middle childhood, one of the most common problems among sisters is the fear of sibling contamination, which usually manifests in a case of the cooties.

For many decades, parents and psychologists have wondered, "What exactly are the cooties? How are they transmitted? Is there a cure?"

The assumption that a sibling possesses cooties is related to an unconscious fear that a sister's major personality flaws may be hereditary. Thus, a prime question sisters ask is, "If my sister's a geek, am I doomed?"

The only defense is the time-honored practice of spraying the cootie victim with invisible cootie spray.

The technique involves holding up an invisible aerosol can and emitting a hissing sound by whistling through the teeth. At the same time, the sprayer may also exclaim, "Spraying for cooties!"

The desired result of the cootie defense is to humiliate the cootie-infested sibling and send her crying to Mommy.

Although cootie spraying has historically proven remarkably effective, in recent years, some states have placed severe restrictions on the practice. In deference to our decaying ozone layer, cootie spraying has been all but outlawed in most of the blue states, Alaska, and parts of the Virgin Islands.

Pending legislation may obliterate the practice in several other parts of the country as well.

Concerned environmentalists promote a more ozone-friendly solution to sibling contamination. The organization STOP (Save the Ozone, Please!) has been lobbying against cootie spraying since the late 1980s. STOP guidelines advise children to avoid the invisible aerosol can.

If forced to occupy the same space, such as the back seat of the family car, STOP recommends drawing an invisible boundary line to prevent the spread of cooties. "Always carry a piece of invisible chalk in your pocket for such emergencies," advises STOP president Merrill Barkow. Siblings should carefully delineate their individual territories, and if a sibling's arm or leg happens to cross this boundary line, it is permissible to interrupt the family game of License Plates or State Capitals by hair-pulling or raucous screaming.

A more permanent and effective STOP defense tactic is for siblings to separate themselves with certifiable proof that they are completely different from their sibling. This is achieved by hanging out with different types of kids and participating in different activities. One child may claim a sport—gymnastics or wrestling—and devote all of his or her energies to excelling in that sport. One sister may study hard and become the geek of the family. Another sister may take up acting. A third may eat everything in sight and become the child with a weight problem.

In the next section we will explore the various roles children assume to avoid sibling contamination and to establish separate but distinct personalities from each other so that they can pretend that there is no such thing as heredity.

Establishing Your Place in the Family

Almost from birth, you learn to assert your identity by assuming particular personality traits. This is necessary in order to establish your separateness from your siblings, especially since your mother is always calling you by your sister's name.

So, you are either Miss Popularity or the Spoiled Brat, the Reliable Child or the Flake, the Obsessive-Compulsive or the Hypo. These labels make it easier for your parents to remember who you are, especially after a long hard day at the office. Unfortunately, these labels stay with you long after you are grown and have children of your own.

Many studies have been done to define the different routes a child can take in her emotional development. In my research I have discovered that there are eleven roles that children assume in order to establish their place in the family structure. (This research greatly disappointed me as I was hoping for an even dozen.)

Read the following list to determine:
Which are you?
Which one is your sister?

1. Miss Responsibility

This sister is always left in charge of her siblings when Mom and Dad play poker at the Schneiders' on Saturday night. She is the child who will know what to do when a stranger knocks on the door (Don't answer!) or if brother Kevin stays up until midnight reading the dirty magazines he found under Daddy's side of the mattress. (Collect $5 or tell Mommy in the morning.) Other siblings refer to her as the Narc. Most times, but not always, Miss Responsibility is the first-born child. Supremely confident, she often rushes to conclusions and her general credo is "Ready! Fire! Aim!" In later life, it often comes as a shock to her to discover there is not necessarily a reservation in heaven for those who always empty the dishwasher.

2. Miss Smarty Pants

This child excels in school. She works hard, gets good grades, and is promoted as a role model to her fellow siblings by her parents.

She is often asked to assist with her sister's homework or with Dad's weekly sales reports.

Also known as the Teacher's Pet, Miss S. Pants never has the time or inclination to Rollerblade, ride a bike, or join in any activity that involves a ball, a motor skill, or a teammate. She is rarely very popular with other kids. She is prone to writing reams of unmetered poetry and seeing a lot of Saturday afternoon matinees. In later life, she will excel in computer science, medicine, or law. She will make a lot of money and often be hit up for loans from siblings or parents. Though a prim and conservative dresser, she will always harbor a secret fantasy to be Celine Dion.

3. Miss Popularity

The phone never stops ringing for this girl. She uses her charm and good cheer to win friends and influence teachers. She is popular everywhere she goes, except among her sisters.

Miss Popularity will probably marry young and have children before any of her siblings. She will think of herself as the lucky one in the family, at least until the advent of stretch marks. In later years, she will study Kaballah and keep her plastic surgeon on speed dial.

4. Miss Social Butterfly

As opposed to Miss Popularity, Miss Social Butterfly organizes a lot of events, or at least decorates the gym for them. She is away from the house a lot but the phone never rings for her, a situation that only makes her work harder. She will join every club, run for every office, collect stray animals, volunteer in soup kitchens, and needlepoint personalized Christmas stockings for everyone she knows, including her Jewish friends.

Miss Social Butterfly believes in astrology, poignant comic strips, and sending a Hallmark card for every occasion. In later life, she will frequent singles bars, be a compulsive speed dater, vacation at Club Med, and be the first person in her apartment building to get TiVo.

5. Miss Super-Organized

Often isolated from the rest of the family, the organized child is a real drag to share a bathroom with, as she will insist that all hair-care products be aligned by height. She believes that everything in life has a place. When she visits your dorm room, she will alphabetize your CDs.

As an adult, the organized child succeeds famously in corporate life, usually at the expense of her social life. She will own a co-op, sleep in a bed roll to save bed-making time in the morning, organize her Tupperware by lid size, and, in private, register with every computer dating service on the net.

6. Miss Hypo

She whines, she moans, she gets headaches and cramps. She is the first to catch "that twenty-four-hour stomach thing that is going around" and the last to recover from it. She is often bloated.

She will marry rich and divorce early. She will complain bitterly about PMS, alimony, and hot flashes.

7. Miss Flake

Very early in life, Miss Flake realizes that if she leaves her toys and clothes on the floor, someone else will eventually pick them up. After that, she is relatively useless to her siblings, except during the late adolescent years when she will be the best source for illicit drugs.

Miss Flake will experiment with sex at an early age and get very good at it. She will be attracted to men who have tattoos and ride motorcycles. She will marry often and have many children who will grow up to be surprisingly adept at taking care of her.

8. Miss Klutz

She trips, she stumbles, she falls. She stubs her toe, knocks over the milk, drops the dishes, and burns herself whenever she tries to bake. She is a walking disaster; her nails are constantly chipped. She goes through life with Band-Aids on her knees and Ace bandages around her ankles. She constantly apologizes for her clumsiness and then breaks your favorite Disney figurine.

Oddly enough, she dreams of being a ballerina, a Dallas cheerleader, or a dental hygienist. In later life, she will get into many fender benders and may develop agoraphobia. Most likely, she will be a wedding planner and, in her spare time, sell useless stuff on eBay.

9. Miss Tomboy

The complete opposite of Miss Klutz, Miss Tomboy will excel in every sport. She plays kickball with a vengeance, tennis like a pro, and basketball until she actually sweats. She will be the first one picked for any team sport.

She plays catch with Dad and prides herself on never having thrown a softball underhand. She will fall in love with her junior high school gym teacher and never wash her gym shorts. In later life, she will wear comfortable shoes no matter what the occasion.

10. Miss Spoiled Brat

Usually the youngest, the Spoiled Brat is babied most of her life by other members of the family. All of her needs are met and all of her desires fulfilled, if not by her parents then by her siblings. The Spoiled Brat does not think of herself as spoiled; she believes she is getting only what she rightfully deserves in life.

As an adult, she will have an American Express Platinum Card and very expensive lingerie, and she will order take-out three nights a week. Throughout her life, she will think it a compliment when people call her a princess.

11. Miss Miscellaneous

This is the catchall category for those sisters born at the bottom of a large sibling heap. Pity poor Miss Miscellaneous!

Like most younger siblings from big families, Miss Miscellaneous is confounded to discover, at around age twelve, that all of the really good personalities are taken.

Such was the case for Elizabeth W., the youngest of twelve children. Elizabeth's older siblings had staked out almost every possible alternative. Her sisters and brothers had already assumed generic positions as the Brain, the Athlete, the Juvenile Delinquent, the Geek, the Beauty, the Bookworm, the Dancer, the Nincompoop, the Actress, the Computer Genius, and the Slut. Elizabeth, a desperate but remarkably resourceful Miss Miscellaneous, developed a fascination for embalming and taxidermy, which she practiced on the innumerable family pets that came (and went) through the course of her childhood.

Other Miss Miscellaneous siblings have been known to excel at Yahtzee, collect Martha Stewart magazines, and have unusual but grandiose allergies.

Teen Sisters:

The Lipstick Wars

Remember that as a teenager you are at the last stage in your life when you will be happy to hear that the phone is for you.

Fran Lebowitz

Learning to Share
and Other Contradictions

For a sibling of any age or economic status, nothing is more painful, confusing, or difficult to grasp than the concept of sharing. "You must share everything," parents tell their children, "but you cannot play with Mommy's things or touch Daddy's desk."

At an early age, children accept the idea that they must share their stuff with classmates or kids in the neighborhood. They do this, however unwillingly, because if they don't, they won't have any friends. Thus, sharing becomes the logical means to an important end. But the point of sharing anything with a sibling is difficult, if not impossible, for the child to comprehend. A kid's sense of logic runs along these lines: My sister will always be my sister, no matter how badly I treat her, so why bother sacrificing anything?

"Why should I be nice to *her*?" sisters want to know. "What's in it for me?"

The situation is complicated by the fact that sharing with a sibling is not only a matter of taking turns with the kickball or waiting in line at the water fountain, sibling sharing goes far beyond these small acts of courtesy and generosity.

Here is what parents require of sisters: You must share your playthings, your bedroom, your meals, your bath, your bedtime, your friends, your family, your iPod, your cell phone, your school, your teachers, your vacations, your punishments, your rewards, your dog, your computer, your life, liberty, and pursuit of happiness—all without showing any signs of jealousy, resentment, or envy.

Here's what children wonder: Are my parents crazy or what?

The answer is no, they're not crazy. From the very beginning, your parents actually intended to do the very best job of parenting they possibly could—which only makes it all the more astounding how they managed to muck up everything.

Before you were born, Mom probably harbored the illusion that you and your sister would always be kind, loving, and generous with each other. She might even tell you one day that she decided to have a second child so that there would be two of you to share everything. Mom had this fantasy that you two would be best friends, date each other's friends and, perhaps, even insist on a double wedding. She conveniently disregarded the fact that she and her sister fought like dogs and cats when they were children and did not speak to each other from May 1986 to January 1992.

This is just part of the confusion of parenting. You

want your daughter to have everything but you don't want to spoil her. You want her to learn from your own years of experience without actually having to go through the same experiences herself. You want her life to be perfect even though you know, for sure, that there is no such thing as a perfect life.

Because of such confusion, mothers are often ambiguous and contradictory in the rules they lay down for their daughters. They tend to forget all the advice they read in books or hear from Dr. Phil and make everything up as they go along. This results in many inconsistencies.

The following are only a sampling of the hopelessly contradictory rules mothers try to instill in their daughters.

Mom's Mixed Messages

1. Be completely loyal to each other but always rat each out when I want to know who is responsible for the mess.

2. Be very, very close but completely different.

3. Be competitive but never fight.

4. Be tolerant and kind to your sister but don't let her get away with anything when I am out of the house.

5. Be aggressive in getting what you want and in sports but don't hurt each other.

6. Cooperate with each other but do everything my way.

7. Enjoy playing together but no running in the house, no fingerprints on the wall, and give the remote to me.

The truth is that we share stuff with our sister because Mom wouldn't let us have anything at all if we didn't. But that does not mean we have to like it.

Despite what Mom says, this is not selfishness per se. It is human nature to be possessive. Why else does Mom have to own every piece of green Depression glass ever displayed on a thrift shop shelf?

Some sisters are better at pretending to share than others, but for the majority, if sisters were really free to express their innermost feelings, Mom would hear this: "Give me all the attention and all the toys and send Rebecca to live with Grandma."

Sharing and Competing

The roots of selfishness can be traced to the earliest stages of life. Almost from birth, you and your siblings are lumped together in one package. Instead of your former life as "our darling baby girl Jessica;" you are now part of an ensemble called "the kids," "the girls," or "the children."

This sets the stage for sibling competition. Upon this stage, almost anything can be the basis for a dispute. Siblings have been known to argue over toys, clothes, who gets the biggest piece of candy, which TV shows to watch, who gets to sit in the front seat, who gets to be a witch at Halloween, and who gets to be the most in love with the most recent *American Idol*, among many many other things, events, people, and situations.

Though parents may argue that their children must "share and share alike," even the densest mom or dad knows that we live in a competitive world and the sooner the kids learn to deal with competition, the more stuff they can start accumulating in life. As my Mom used to tell me: "Every day, someone is out there working a little bit harder than you, earning a little bit more money, so that he or she can buy a BMW while your lazy father is still driving a 1986 Honda."

So, too, kids learn at an early age that the one with the most PlayStation games gets more friends to come over after school. A kid living in a bedroom filled with computer games, a forty-two-inch flat screen TV, and seventy-two different shades of nail polish gets to tell her friends, "I'm somebody. Mom and Dad spent a fortune on me. What have you got to show for yourself?"

How to Get Your Piece of the Parental Purse

There is an old saying: "The squeaky wheel gets the grease." This rule also applies in childhood. As most parents will reluctantly acknowledge, "The whiny kid gets the ten-speed bike."

It's a simple law of family life that a parent can only withstand a finite amount of whining. Thus, children learn, early enough, that begging, pleading, and praying out loud can be a goal-oriented means of material gain.

In a competitive environment, such as the dinner table, children often employ attention-generating methods such as giggling, throwing food, and banging feet. While these techniques are effective in gaining parental attention, they can also backfire and get you dismissed from the table before dessert.

Children also discover the benefit of sacrificing a sibling for personal gain. Thus, Sasha will feel compelled to tell Mom and Dad that sister Debbie was seen necking in the basement with Duncan Carey after school. While Sasha is surely risking the threat of sibling retribution, the thrill of seeing her parents' reaction may offset her fears. Also, and even more important, Sasha knows that while Mom and Dad are lecturing Debbie about hanging out with hoodlums, they are unlikely to inquire about the algebra test Sasha took that morning.

Alternative Modes of Sibling Torture

Adolescence is a time in childhood development when siblings begin to express themselves through alternative means. For this reason, parents often call the advent of adolescence "The Reign of Terror" and with good cause. The teen years represent the era when sisters learn and refine various techniques for browbeating each other.

1. Bickering

The language mode most commonly used between siblings is called bickering. A careful blend of sarcasm, irony, teasing, and downright insults, bickering has its own distinctive cadence and rhythm and is as difficult to master as Chinese. The fine points can only be discerned in the subtle rise and fall of the voice. If not practiced properly, bickering can be mistaken for its less sophisticated counterpart, whining.

Like a great game of chess or tennis, bickering is a delicate interplay of point/counterpoint. One well-modulated insult breeds another, then another and so on. Needling may be employed. Time-out is called when one sister turns crybaby and retreats.

2. Fighting

This is always a favorite, especially among the older, stronger, and more powerful sibling. Methods include biting, kicking, scratching, hair pulling, or any other means that recklessly disregards a sibling's well-being.

Children soon discover that the only central commandment when physically abusing a sibling is not to attack the general head area. From an early age, they are reminded of the most sacred parental admonishment: "You could poke out an eye!" Since parents never say, "You could poke out a collarbone" or "You could poke out your sister's pituitary gland," children learn that any body part other than the eyeball is fair game.

Most sibling fights are terminated by the arrival of a parent, guardian, babysitter, or law enforcement official. An adult will try to break up the argument with the maturity and calmness that comes with age. A child really learns something about anger management when hearing an adult they admire scream, "I don't care who started it—you both go to your rooms and get the hell out of my sight. If I hear you fighting again, I'm going to kick the crap out of both of you!"

Of course, fighting is a fairly normal way that children work through their differences. The conflict can, however, be said to have gotten out of control if it involves poison, attempted drowning, and/or setting a sibling on fire. Then it is time to call in Supernanny.

3. Verbal Abuse

Name calling, taunting, curse words, and feral teasing are the main aspects of verbal abuse between siblings. As annoying as this method may be when you are living in the bedroom down the hall, it has been noted that prolonged verbal abuse can help increase vocabulary, diction, and voice projection.

4. The Copycat

Here is a truly effective method of sibling torture that is especially popular among younger siblings. Older siblings may possess the strength to overpower, but when it comes to being annoying and irritating, younger siblings definitely have the edge. This method involves repeating everything a sibling says. Over and over and over again. While seemingly innocuous, the Copycat Method has been known to drive older siblings over the brink of sanity. No one in their right mind can bear to hear their own words repeated and thrown back at them for hours on end.

5. The Most Effective Torture Method

Aside from locking a sibling in a room and forcing her to listen continuously to Christina Aguilera, there is one surefire method for torturing a sibling: totally ignore her!

While siblings can take a fair amount of abuse—egos are resilient and broken bones do heal—no one can tolerate being ignored.

6. Combination Platter

Most siblings learn early enough to employ all five methods of sibling torture. Many siblings have had great success by combining them into an endless loop. The cycle involves four easy steps.

a. Relentlessly bicker and tease your sister until she gets mad enough to strike back.

b. Copy everything she says and does.

c. Either use your superior strength to bring her to her knees or your speed to get out of her way.

d. When she finally catches you, go totally limp and ignore her completely.

Teaching Your Sister About S-E-X

Sisters have always served as role models to their siblings for learning about sex and sexual behavior. We find documentation way back in ancient times in such cultural phenomena as the song "I Wish I Could Shimmy Like My Sister Kate!"

As has already been discussed in previous chapters, siblings teach each other about jealousy, rivalry, rage, and envy; these are the same basic default emotions we all employ when we start having relationships with members of the opposite sex.

Other aspects of human sexuality become known through sibling relationships. How we dress, for example, is an important barometer of our sexuality and how we feel about ourselves. We can learn a lot about children by being sensitive to their habits and manners. When a sister asks to borrow her older sister's cashmere sweater, she is saying that she admires and wants to look like her sister. When a sister takes her younger sister's favorite pair of suede shoes, without asking, and then carelessly ruins them by wearing them in the rain, she is saying, in effect, "I'm selfish, so what?" And when a younger brother asks to wear his sister's strapless prom dress, he is telling us, in so many words, "When I grow up, I want to be J-Lo."

An older sister can have enormous influence over a younger sister. She may teach her how to apply lipstick, how to breathe when kissing, when to "go steady." She can show her sister how to gracefully turn down a date, avoid a boy's advances, and when to say, "Stop that or I will kick you where it really really hurts!"

Parents who are uncomfortable talking about sex with their children often rely on older siblings to pass along information. Before parents feel too secure about passing along this responsibility, they should realize that the older sister can, and probably will, also teach their younger siblings about French kissing, hickies, smoking, drinking, making out, stealing money from Mom's purse, taking Dad's car keys, smoking pot, and experimenting with various illegal substances.

Thus, sisters can have a negative influence on their younger counterparts. When should you stop using your sister as a role model? If you suspect that your sister is the town tramp then ignore her advice and, for heaven's sake, do not borrow her underwear.

Adult Sisters:

The Days of Salad Bars and Nail Salons

"My sister's wedding" was right up there with "my recent colostomy" in terms of three-word phrases I hoped never to use.

David Sedaris,
Naked

Advice for Surviving Your Sister's Wedding

For single women, weddings can be a $50,000 reminder that all the good guys are taken.

Nothing on the planet is more intimidating to a single woman than receiving a wedding invitation and seeing, next to her name on the envelope, the two most dreaded words in all of unmarried life: "And Escort."

Nausea sets in immediately.

The only thing more catastrophic and troubling is if the wedding is for your younger sister, so here are some thoughts and advice for muddling your way through such an appalling event.

~

Do not panic! Remind yourself that there are worse things in life. You are a survivor! You made it through high school, didn't you?

~

If you don't have a steady guy, your first inclination will be to find an ex-boyfriend who might be willing to escort you to the wedding. Try to avoid this frustrating exercise at all costs. Trust me on this: You are bound to discover that every guy you ever dated got married three months after he broke up with you.

~

It is possible that your best guy friend can be persuaded to be your escort. However, you should be forewarned that it is most likely he will run off with one of the more attractive bridesmaids, leaving you alone to deal with Uncle Howie and Aunt Miriam whining about wanting to dance at *your* wedding.

~

The need to have an escort for your sister's wedding is, I believe, one the primary reasons for the invention of gay men. To wit, gay men look fabulous in formal clothes, they are almost always great dancers, and they can be funny and generous with the family members that you cannot stomach for more than two minutes and thirty seconds.

~

A number of Hollywood movies begin with the concept of a single woman hiring a gorgeous male escort for her sister's wedding. While this may work on the silver screen, unless you look like Debra Messing or Julia Roberts or Kelly Lynch, this is probably not a good idea. And besides, escort services charge a fortune! You should see my MasterCard bill!

~

A word about shower gifts: What really irritates single women is that no ever thinks to buy us cheese trays with matching knives, silver frames, or ice buckets. Why not? We like cheese. We use ice in our drinks. We even enjoy something monogrammed every now and then. Sometimes I think it's worth getting engaged just for the gifts. As a wise woman, engaged three times, once told me: "The guy can be returned but the gifts definitely last forever, especially those that come in sterling silver."

~

As your sister's maid of honor, your job is to throw her a shower, make sure her train is properly unfurled, help her with the veil, hold her bouquet, keep Mom from driving her crazy, and pretend you are *not* secretly hoping she will trip over her feet while walking down the aisle.

~

After the ceremony, it is permissible to get a headache and leave before the reception, especially if your sister was a cheerleader in school and you were the one with a weight problem.

~

Try to avoid the wedding photographs. In years to come, these will be depressing reminders of your single life.

~

Drink heavily. And remember, this is no time to abstain from your drug of choice.

~

Try to be nice to the groom, your future brother-in-law. Keep in mind that in the years to come, you will be feeding him at Thanksgiving and learning all the intimate details of his sexual inadequacies from your sister. (Sometimes *during* Thanksgiving dinner!) And no matter how lavish the wedding reception or how much your sister flaunts her diamond ring in your face, in the future, you will be first-hand witness to all the ways he will disappoint her as their marriage progresses.

~

You will be obligated to deliver the traditional first toast to the bride and groom. Do not include any references to your sister's previous boyfriends, her addictions, or her skin problems.

~

When the orchestra strikes up the music for the couple's first dance, make your way to the ladies' room and stay there for at least an hour or so. (This is why I always recommend that a well-prepared maid of honor bring a good novel or *People* magazine to her sister's wedding.) After the first fifteen minutes of dancing, the guests will start feeling the effects of their alcohol consumption and no one will notice that you don't have a dance partner.

~

There is no escaping the traditional bouquet toss so go for it! Despite your disgust at the ridiculous ritual of wedding ceremonies, you will find yourself leaping for the bouquet, just in case. . . .

Fourteen Surefire Ways to Drive Your Adult Sister Crazy

1. Tell her, "You're just like Mom."

2. Forget her birthday.

3. Remind her of the time she split her pants on the ski slope, didn't get invited to the spring dance, flunked gym, got stood up, etc. This is particularly effective if you have this conversation in mixed company, say, when her new boyfriend arrives for his first dinner with the family, during a cocktail party for her boss, or in front of her children.

4. Tell her that her special tuna casserole gave you gas.

5. Have a best friend.

6. Marry a man she can't stand.

7. After you've been in therapy for more than a year and your sister wants to know what you told your shrink about her, say, "Actually I don't think I ever mentioned you." Smile sweetly.

8. Dress better than she does.

9. Lose weight.

10. Get a big promotion and make her take you out to celebrate.

11. Brag about your rip-roaring sex life.

12. Wear expensive shoes.

13. Borrow the family heirlooms from Mom (silverware, diamond necklace, Grandma's lace tablecloth) and keep them.

14. Have perfect hair.

Dear Linda,

My sister has been kind of depressed and her birthday is coming soon. What can I get to cheer her up?

Betsy

Dear Betsy,

For my sister's last birthday, I got her boxed sets of the complete first, second, third, and fourth seasons of <u>The West Wing</u>. She was really depressed at the time and the gift gave her the excuse to spend sixty-four hours watching television, a personal best for her and second place only to her husband, who has been known to lay prone on the couch for an entire month with only short breaks for the bathroom, the refrigerator, and the computer.

Of course, it is her husband's capacity to never get up off the couch and his enthusiasm for sports that made my sister depressed in the first place, but at least she is no longer sleeping fourteen hours a night.

Now she has a mad crush on Martin Sheen and Allison Janney and her spirits are high. The new <u>West Wing</u> season starts next month so she says she finally has something to live for!

Linda

Why Your Sister's Grass Is Always Greener and Her Carpet Is Always Cleaner

As adults, we know very little about how our sisters actually function in the real world. Somehow our sister's life seems so much better than our own, especially if she got invited to the junior prom while she was still a sophomore and you did not. If you thought your sister was the most popular girl in junior high, you will keep this misconception well into adulthood, even if she has not had a real relationship since Demi Moore dated men her own age.

Once sisters grow up and pursue different lifestyles, their mutual misconceptions about each other become entrenched. This is especially true if one sister marries and the other stays single. Single women tend to have unrealistic expectations of married life (which may be one reason why they stay single.) Conversely, once a woman marries, she often forgets the hardships of single life and indulges in some creative rewriting of her own personal history. Thus, sisters of differing marital status have trouble understanding each other's daily life.

To illustrate this point, I asked the Rheinhold sisters from Rockport, Rhode Island, to tell me—in intimate detail—how they each imagined a typical weekend in her sister's life. After receiving these essays, I asked each sister to review what her sibling had written and to comment on how close her sister's fantasy fits the reality of her life.

The results of this experiment may shock and disarm you, but not half as much as they shocked and disarmed the sisters' mother.

A Single Woman's Fantasy of Her Married Sister's Weekend

My sister, Lucky, is married to the perfect man—an investment banker—who looks like a cross between George Stephanopoulos and that Nate character on *Six Feet Under*. My brother-in-law loves to slow dance at family weddings and he is a wonderful cook. I nicknamed him Rhett because he has a very sexy southern accent.

The following is how I envision a typical weekend at their lovely home—an enormous McMansion in the suburbs of Chicago.

FRIDAY AFTERNOON: Lucky spends the day organizing a charity event for homeless women at an exclusive club on Lake Shore Drive. After lunch with her best friend from college and a quick shopping trip to Saks for an evening gown for the charity event, she hurries home, anxious to see her three adorable children, Joshua (ten), Jared (six), and Jennifer (four), and her live-in maid, Conceptia (twenty-three). The kids look like Ralph Lauren models and act like little angels. Conceptia speaks perfect English, never wants a day off, and enjoys washing windows in her spare time. Lucky is so sure of her husband that she never minds his flirting with Conceptia. (In Spanish!)

When Lucky arrives home, the children are returning from their school for gifted children. Lucky asks what they learned that day. Joshua explains the basic principles of algebra, Jared recites a poem by Walt Whitman, and the baby, Jennifer, answers in Japanese.

Everyone changes clothes and spends quality time together while Conceptia prepares a gourmet dinner.

Rhett returns home from his office in time to play ball with the boys, work on a dollhouse he is building for Jennifer, repair a leaky faucet in the laundry room, and massage Lucky's feet.

Rhett insists that she take a bubble bath while he helps feed, bathe, and get the children ready for bed. Refreshed from her bath, Lucky offers to read a bedtime story to the boys who select a very thin book with only two sentences per page. By page six, the children are fast asleep.

Then Rhett and Lucky share a candlelit champagne dinner. They dance to the sound track from *Ray*. He gives her two dozen white roses he has stashed in the garage refrigerator because tonight is the twelfth anniversary of the day they first met. Lucky reminds him that their wedding anniversary is only two weeks away. He promises to buy her a new car.

He waltzes her upstairs to the master suite where they make love three times and fall asleep locked in each other's arms. Neither one of them snores.

Meanwhile, Conceptia is in the kitchen, waxing the floors and polishing the silverware.

SATURDAY MORNING: The children play quietly in their rooms until Mommy and Daddy wake up.

After breakfast, the family piles into the Volvo station

wagon (last year's anniversary present) for a drive to the country. On the way, they pass a garage sale in progress and, knowing how much Mom loves a bargain, everyone eagerly agrees to stop. Lucky finds a complete and original set of Fiestaware, in assorted colors and perfect condition, for $35. She bargains with the owner and gets the price down to $15.

That night, Lucky decides to cook her favorite stir-fry dish so Rhett volunteers to go shopping at the local market and then washes, slices, and dices seven different vegetables. Then he does the dishes.

After the kids are asleep, Rhett joins Lucky for a long talk in front of a roaring fire. He listens attentively to all her problems, calms her fears and anxieties, vows to love her for all eternity and set up an independent trust fund for her and the children that will support them well into the next century.

SUNDAY: Rhett insists on cooking breakfast for the kids and serving Lucky breakfast in bed. The whole family climbs into their massive king-sized bed. No one spills anything or gets any crumbs on the bedspread.

Joshua discusses a personal problem with his parents, listens attentively to their opinions, and then thanks them for their advice.

At noon, the children are picked up by their grandparents so that Lucky and Rhett can spend the day together by themselves. They drive into the city to their favorite little sidewalk café where they sit all afternoon holding hands, stealing kisses, whispering in each other's ears, and giggling like two teenagers in love. Watching all the people in the street, Lucky starts counting all the miserable single women that she sees walk by. By the time she reaches 487, she's ready to return home.

That night, the kids insist on watching PBS. During a pledge break, the *Chicago Sun Times* calls to tell Lucky that she has been voted Best Mom in the Midwest and her photo will appear on the front page of tomorrow's paper.

Lucky squeals with delight. This weekend was almost as good as the one when she won the Illinois State Lottery.

A Married Sister Responds

First of all, for the record, children look like models and act like angels only when they are fast asleep. And husbands never make love more than once a night, if ever. Who gave my sister these ideas? And when can I meet him?

It's true that my husband is an investment banker but, also true, he was heavily invested in the dot-com market and is now in debt up to his eyeballs. Yes, we live in a McMansion, which also means I have thirteen toilets that need to be scrubbed. My husband does like to dance at family weddings but only with young ladies under the age of twenty. And no, I don't have to worry about him flirting with Conceptia because she weighs 250 pounds and has a crush on Rosie O'Donnell.

It is true that a mate will chop veggies for stir-fry although he will refuse to do the dishes. He will hug you before you go to sleep, especially if he does not want to have sex that night. And a husband will tell you that you are not fat (at least mine will and my sister can't have him) when you think you are so fat that you deserve to die.

I should add, though, that a live-in maid can either cook or speak English but never both. No one can even look at Fiestaware for under $200. My children never ask for my opinion and have never said thank you for anything. And I am flattered but I never won a Best Mom award, even from my own kids, or the Illinois State Lottery, though I once found a ten-dollar bill in the ladies' room at Saks.

Honestly, if my life was half as peaceful or ran as smoothly as my sister thinks, I would not be living on Valium and twelve cups of coffee a day.

A Married Sister's Fantasy of Her Single Sister's Weekend

My sister doesn't know that she is the kind of woman that everyone envies—tall, nice legs, quirky sense of style, great hair. She has a master's in American Studies from Cornell and a Marc Jacobs wardrobe. She writes chick-lit novels that sell like crazy and travels all over the world. I'll bet she has a guy in every city, and some suburbs as well. She's thirty-two, looks twenty-five, and is too happy to even think about settling down. Call her Scarlett.

FRIDAY EVENING: Scarlett takes a ballet class after work. Dancing is her hobby and she actually enjoys exercising. Can you imagine? After class, she attends a concert at Lincoln Center. She could've invited one of her numerous friends—the tickets are one of many perks from magazine editors who are begging her to write for them—but after a week of city hubbub, appointments cross-town, and deadlines, she glories in being alone, a privilege her married-with-kids friends experience only in the bathroom (and sometimes not even then).

Walking home, Scarlett hums Mozart and thinks about her long-distance lover, Brian, a much-acclaimed architect and mountain climber whose work and hobby take him around the globe. Tomorrow he will interrupt an important weekend conference to spend twenty-four hours with her in New York City. They haven't been together in weeks and won't see each other for at least a month when they'll spend five days together at the Four Seasons in Los Angeles. Scarlett loves this arrangement: She's attached but not obligated and, in her humble opinion, the room service at the L.A. Four Seasons is the best in the country.

SATURDAY: After sleeping soundly until noon, Scarlett takes a yoga class and then has a massage and sauna. Her time and money are her own so she also gets her hair highlighted, her nails done, and a pedicure. Afterward she shops at Jimmy Choo and then picks up cold lobster salad, avocados, grapes, imported cheese, and a bottle of French wine at a gourmet food store on Fifty-seventh Street.

Arriving home, Scarlett drops all her shopping bags on the island kitchen counter in the waterfront loft she bought several years before the real estate boom. Her decorating style is softly minimalist with only a few choice pieces of white furniture and a huge platform bed where she sleeps on silk sheets and satin pillows.

She dresses slowly and carefully in a stunning Audrey Hepburn–style black cocktail dress and when the doorbell rings, she runs, barefoot, to answer it.

"Hello, love!" Brian exclaims as he rushes to embrace her. He easily lifts her off the ground and twirls her around the room.

Over dinner, he asks her to spend Christmas with him in Greece. "Maybe," she demurs. "Perhaps I can be persuaded if you rent that little villa overlooking the sea where we spent Valentine's last year."

SUNDAY: Brian leaves in the late afternoon. Scarlett thinks about him as she sits in the sexy disarray of her bed, dressed in a pale blue nightgown, one of a half dozen pieces of lacy lingerie he brought her from Paris. Scribbling notes for her latest novel, she sips peppermint tea. Then she calls her best friend, Lena, and they decide to see the new Bill Murray movie that night. After the film, they head toward their favorite neighborhood bistro to discuss, review, and analyze their respective Saturday night dates.

As they talk, they are being watched by two men who are drinking beer in a corner booth. Scarlett looks up and recognizes one of the men as a fairly well-known painter; last week she attended an opening of his work where she saw him looking at her. They never met because he was surrounded by a mob of photographers and well-wishers and she was already late for a dinner date uptown. She wonders if he remembers her from then.

He notices her glance at him, smiles, and walks over to her table. He's tall and broad, with dark eyes and a reddish beard.

"Hello," he says, revealing an intriguing accent. "My name is Anton Orloff."

"I know," Scarlett grins.

He returns the smile; his teeth are very white. "I am very happy to be meeting with you at this longing last."

"I'm very happy to meet you, too," Scarlett answers with a giggle. And she is. At this longing last.

A Single Sister Responds

I thought my sister got everything exactly right but then, as my shrink used to say, I live in a fantasy world. So I showed the essay to my shrink. She said, "Boy, it has been a long time since your sister was single, eh?" Together, during my last session, we discussed some inaccuracies. As I am trying hard to move away from my own personal state of denial, I must confess the following:

1. Brian is married.

2. Our trip to Greece got canceled when his wife discovered our plane tickets and threatened to kill herself, him, and me, although not in that order.

3. I never actually finished my thesis so, *technically*, I don't really have a master's, and although my novels do sell well, the critics hate my work and my books are always panned in the *New York Times*.

4. I never sleep till noon on Saturday morning because Mom calls at dawn to ask when I am going to stop wasting my life, settle down, marry a doctor, and have three kids like my sister.

5. The Jimmy Choos give me such blisters that I can't wear them for more than five minutes.

6. My waterfront loft has mice.

7. Anton Orloff turns out to be gay.

Dear Linda,

My sister can afford $600 sunglasses with French labels and Italian shoes that cost the same as my monthly mortgage payment. I try not to be jealous but it is difficult. Thank heavens she has small breasts and wears a size ten shoe or I would not be able to talk to her at all.

Katy

Dear Katy,

My friend Gloria is in the same situation and her sister's wealth would really be a problem if Gloria could not borrow stuff all the time and swim in her sister's pool whenever she wanted.

Personally, I feel that if you can't be rich yourself, it is extremely intelligent to have wealthy friends and/or family members in your life, especially those with summer homes near the ocean.

Linda

Dear Linda,

My sister is a perfectionist. Not as bad as that Monk character on TV but bad enough. She asked her husband to put together a desk she bought at IKEA. According to him it had a "gazillon nuts and bolts" and the instructions were in Swedish. I don't know the particulars but somehow the desk came out with slightly uneven drawers. That was five years ago and my sister still has not forgiven him or stopped talking about it.

I want to smack her in the head. I am so bored hearing the same complaint every time we talk. I mean, my niece, for whom the desk was originally purchased, is now a sophomore in college and is talking about getting married. No one cares about the drawers anymore, except my sister.

Help! How can I shut her up about the damn desk already?

Cheryl

Dear Cheryl,

Oh, for those good old days when you could actually smack your sister in the head, and get away with it—so long as your parents didn't see you do it. As adults, we must modify our behavior or else, in the future, we will all need to hire expensive lawyers to represent us in court and/or spend hours in anger-management classes.

If you really love your sister, though, you will not sabotage her constitutional right to bitch and moan about her husband. In fact, holding a grudge against him might just be the most enjoyable part of her marriage.

My advice is for you to stop getting annoyed when your sister complains about the IKEA desk. And don't worry, this will eventually pass because, in the years and perhaps decades to come, if she stays married to this same guy, she will discover much, much worse stuff to hold against him.

Linda

Timeline of Sisterly Love: The Gabor Girls

Long before the tabloids were filled with stories of Paris and Nicky Hilton, Jessica and Ashlee Simpson and, oh, those skinny Olson twins, the Gabor sisters were the siblings the public wanted most to dish. And boy did those crazy Hungarians give the public what they wanted. Just like the Hilton sisters, the Gabors were beautiful, rich, fashion forward, glamorous, and horny as hell.

The Gabors shared everything: plastic surgeons, publicists, guest appearances, and the occasional husband. They often competed for movie roles that might be played with a Hungarian accent and engaged in well-publicized "feuds" filled with conflict and drama. As their mom, Jolie Gabor, once told the press, "In America, my girls were wealthy, famous, and unhappy. They were most dissatisfied with their men and with each other."

A brief look at the lives of the Gabor girls is therefore a cautionary tale of sibling rivalry and remorse. Witness the following:

1920s (possibly earlier): Magda, Zsa Zsa, and Eva are born to Jolie and Vilmos Gabor in Hungary. Exact years of birth have never been confirmed; in fact, in the decades to come, the girls will claim they were born in the 1930s, meaning they each married, for the first time, at about nine years of age.

1930s: As soon as legally possible, all three sisters are married: Magda to an impoverished Hungarian aristocrat,

Zsa Zsa to a Turkish diplomat, and Eva to a still-in-training Swedish osteopath. All three marriages combust in spontaneous divorces.

1939: Mama Jolie encourages her daughters to move to America. "You will be rich, famous, and married to kings," she tells them. Eva moves to Hollywood to seek a career in the movies.

1942: Zsa Zsa follows Eva to Hollywood, also to pursue a film career, and marries Conrad Hilton, hotel baron, multimillionaire, and future great-grandfather to Paris and Nicky.

1940s: Zsa Zsa becomes addicted to uppers and Eva has her committed. Zsa Zsa tells the press Eva was jealous and reveals that her sister is living in sin with John Perona, owner of the infamous El Morocco Nightclub.[1]

- Magda, in Budapest, has an affair with a Portuguese ambassador who helps her, Mama Jolie, and Dad escape war-torn Hungary.

- Eva marries millionaire Charles Isaacs.

- Magda's arrival in New York is shrouded in mystery. Reporters wait for her dockside but she never appears. According to rumor, Eva and Zsa Zsa have Magda secretly smuggled out of her cabin and rushed by ambulance to a Long Island clinic for an immediate nose job.[2] With a nose compatible to her

---

1. Note to anyone born after 1970: In the 1940s, living with a man without marrying him first was scandalous. Unlike today, cohabitating with a man back then was not considered an extended form of dating.

2. Also hard to believe: Nose jobs, in fact all forms of vanity plastic surgery, were considered private and personal in the 1940s.

sisters, Magda is presented to the New York press.

1946: Zsa Zsa gives birth to Constance Francesca Hilton, the only child born to the Gabor sisters. A few months later she divorces Hilton.

- Magda marries William Rankin, a Hollywood writer and divorces him in 1947.

1949: Zsa Zsa marries character actor George (*All About Eve*) Sanders but they establish separate residences.[3]

- Magda marries Sidney Warren.

1951: Zsa Zsa's career soars after she appears as a panelist on an early TV talk show. She is offered ten movie roles, twenty-five more TV appearances, and national publicity—thus achieving in a half hour what sister Eva had been unable to do in twelve years.[4]

- Though still married to Sanders, Zsa Zsa begins a well-publicized affair with Porfirio Rubirosa of the Dominican Republic, a famous playboy and some-time diplomat, recently divorced from tobacco heiress Doris Duke. During his three-year affair with Zsa Zsa, Porfirio will wed another heiress, Barbara Hutton; their marriage will last for seventy-three days.

1953: All three sisters appear together for the first time at the Frontier Hotel in Las Vegas. Their show is called "The Gabor Sisters—This Is Our Life!" The fact that none of them can sing or dance or even speak proper English does not seem to hinder their popularity.

---

3. Apparently, for the Gabors, living in sin is okay, living with a husband is not.

4. Just imagine how happy this made Eva!

- Mama Jolie insists on joining the act, too.
- Eva warns that she doesn't want to be lumped together with her sisters. "We are not the McGuire sisters," she informs the hotel manager. He replies, "Duh."
- Opening night is disrupted when Zsa Zsa arrives with a black eye, courtesy of Porfirio. Mama Jolie, Eva, and Magda are furious about the subsequent embarrassing publicity.

1954: Zsa Zsa divorces George Sanders. "Married life with Zsa Zsa was one of the great humiliations of my life," he later tells reporters.

1955: Magda attempts suicide with an overdose of sleeping pills after being dumped by her boyfriend, Tony Gallucci.

1956: Eva marries Dr. John Williams, a plastic surgeon. In October, she divorces him, has an affair with actor Tyrone Power, and in 1959 marries Richard Brown.[5]

- Magda marries Tony Gallucci.

1960s–1980s: Zsa Zsa marries and divorces Herbert Hutner, financial consultant; Joshua Cosden, oil baron; Jack Ryan, inventor associated with both the Barbie and Chatty Cathy dolls; and Mike O'Hara, lawyer. Who says blondes don't have more fun?

On a TV talk show, Zsa Zsa is quoted as saying, "How many husbands have I had? You mean other than my own?"

1967: Magda's husband Tony Gallucci dies, and she suffers

---

5. And all this *before* the advent of computer dating!

a stroke. Nursed slowly back to health, she fights for and wins a substantial portion of Gallucci's estate, becoming the richest Gabor sister.[6]

1967–1972: Eva finally achieves recognition, fame, and fortune from her starring role in the popular TV series, *Green Acres*. Her husband, Richard Brown, is made an executive of the show. She divorces him in 1972.

1970: Magda marries actor George (*All About Eve*) Sanders. Yes, her sister Zsa Zsa's ex! They divorce six weeks later, setting the Gabor record for the shortest marriage. Later, Sanders would say that dealing with the three sisters was "like confronting the Spanish Armada in a rowboat." He commits suicide in 1972, at age sixty-five. The same year, Magda marries Tibor Heltai.

1973: Eva marries Frank Gard Jameson.

- Magda divorces Tibor Heltai.

1976: Zsa Zsa and Eva appear together on the Chicago stage as the murderous sisters in *Arsenic and Old Lace*.[7]

1982: Zsa Zsa marries Felipe de Alba but the marriage is annulled one day later when Zsa Zsa remembers that she is still married to Michael O'Hara.[8]

1980s: Magda, Zsa Zsa, Eva, and Mama Jolie make their home base in Palm Springs, California. Although they do not live together, each daughter calls her mother at least once a day.

---

6. One can only imagine how much pain and envy this caused Zsa Zsa and Eva!

7. You have to wonder who had the bigger dressing room.

8. How do you say "bigamist" in Hungarian?

- Eva divorces Frank Gard Jameson.
- Zsa Zsa marries Frederick Prinz von Anhalt and though she often asks to be called Princess of Anhalt, the truth is that her husband is neither a prince nor royalty. He was born Robert Lichtenberg.
- Zsa Zsa is convicted of three misdemeanor charges as a result of slapping a police officer in the face after he pulled over her car for speeding. The trial (and Zsa Zsa's wardrobe) made national headlines.

1995: Eva, the head of a successful wig company and the author of an autobiography entitled *Orchids and Salami*, dies in Los Angeles after suffering from food poisoning. She is buried in her Rolls Royce car.

1997: Magda, mostly referred to as "the least-known Gabor sister," dies in California.

- Before her death at the age of 97, Mama Jolie proudly tells a reporter, "I like to make from a nothing something."

2005: Zsa Zsa accuses her daughter, Francesa Hilton, of larceny and fraud. The case is still pending in the California courts.

Final Scorecard	
Eva:	5 Husbands
Magda:	6 Husbands
Zsa Zsa:	9 Husbands
TOTAL:	20 Husbands
(21 if you count George Sanders twice)	

Dear Linda,

My sister and I are extremely close and try to spend as much time together as possible. We are devoted to each other and get along famously except during the Jewish holidays when our one area of dispute always becomes a problem: how to cook a brisket.

My sister, Isabelle, insists on a 450° oven and constant basting. I tell her that any fool knows a brisket should be smothered in onions, cooked at 400°, and never basted. Her brisket comes out tough as leather while mine can be cut with a fork.

Still, every holiday she serves that shoe leather and the whole family suffers. Last year, Uncle Sammy nearly choked to death on her brisket. Still, when I generously offered to bring the brisket this year, Isabelle dismissed my suggestion with a laugh. I would try to describe how deeply wounded I was by her remark but the pain is still too deep.

My sister-in-law says I am making too big a deal over this but what the hell does she know? Last time we had the sedar at her house, it was catered by her Irish cook.

If there is any way to resolve this family crisis, I'd like to know it.

Phyllis

Dear Phyllis,

Once sisters become the family caretakers and try to re-create the dinners of their youth, disagreements are bound to ensue. Brisket bickering is typical for Jewish sisters. In other homes, sisters argue over recipes for lasagna, Grandma's corned beef and cabbage, Annie Ruth's fried chicken, or the apple pie that the nanny used to make.

The only solution is to allow each sister her "specialty" dish and for everyone else to just shut up about the outcome of that dish.

Final decisions about basting techniques, the best way to chop an onion, and how many hours it actually takes to roast a turkey should be decided by the person in whose kitchen the meal is prepared. If you are not going to be responsible for cleaning the house before and after the dinner, you should not have final say over the food that is being served.

Linda

Sisters Who Cook Too Much (and Those Who Should!)

In later years, sisters can be defined by their relationship to food and to their participation in the family dinner. Below are several different categories that define the mature sister relationship.

Which one are you? Which one is your sister?

The Zero Food Sister

She is really, really skinny and never brings anything to a family dinner except a bottle of Jack Daniel's, which her husband will polish off before the dessert is served. The Zero Food Sister never eats and thus suffers medical problems such as migraines, stomachaches, and back pains. All of these illnesses are used as an excuse to refrain from contributing any effort to the dinner, including picking up a dinner plate and for once putting it in the sink, heaven forbid.

It would be well for the Zero Food Sister to remember that she is technically still a guest and that her sister's house should be treated like a well-decorated restaurant only if a large tip is left on the table after dessert.

The Soup Sister

The Soup Sister always brings her fabulous chicken noodle soup to the family get-together but, no matter how often she is asked, she will never reveal her recipe. If really pressed she will outright lie and provide a recipe that does not include four or five key ingredients. The Soup Sister knows, deep down, that if she ever gives away her recipe and someone else masters the soup, she may never be invited back.

The Fruit Platter Sister

There is always at least one sister who thinks that bringing a tray of cut fruit straight from the grocery store is the same as spending time actually preparing food. Wrong!

Platters of food prepared in the local grocery or deli or chicken takeout shop are only acceptable for funerals or wakes when the host or hostess is allowed to pull together an impromptu meal. During a wake or after a funeral, no one will be judging you on the food you serve. They will be too busy judging your grief and stress and seeing how well you are holding up.

Cake and Cookies Sister

Baking requires precision and a confident leader who knows what she is doing. A working knowledge of math, especially fractions, is also useful.

Who likes to bake? Control freaks and perfectionists. So baking is usually the domain of the more dominant sister.

The Clean-Up Sister

Sometimes a sister does not like to cook, bake, or shop for food, so she will take on the role of cleaning up the kitchen. These are the very best sisters and are always invited back.

If she is not personally into cleaning, then the Clean-Up Sister can score high marks for paying for maid service.

The What-Are-YOU-Bringing Sister

Yes, she will host Christmas dinner, as long as you bring the ham, your cousin Stephanie makes the salad, and Aunt Cleo bakes the dessert. The What-Are-YOU-Bringing Sister thinks that providing dishes, silverware, and glasses absolves her of actually having to turn on her oven. This sister will usually spend the entire dinner talking about her new car, her recent vacation in the Bahamas, and the ten pounds she absolutely must lose, all the while thinking that everyone else at the table actually cares.

Dear Linda,

My sister and I are both college professors and published authors. We live in university towns and we both lecture frequently. Our secret passion is watching television, especially cop shows. We like to vacation together so that we can watch television for twenty hours a day. Last weekend, we flew to Vegas and spent three days watching the entire first season of <u>Rescue Me</u>. If our colleagues knew about this, we would be laughed out of the intellectual community, but we can't help ourselves. Denis Leary is so cute in those cargo pants.

Anonymous in Vegas

Dear Anonymous in Vegas,

There is no need for you to feel guilty. I am glad you wrote because you bring up a valuable point. It is only with your sister that you can reveal your passion for reality television or your secret crush on Jay Leno.

With your sister, you can stop pretending that you never watch TV! She already knows that deep down you are as shallow as Nicole Richie and Lindsay Lohan. But it does not matter to her! You can relax in your pajamas and discuss the merits of _House_ vs. _Grey's Anatomy_ or _Lost_ vs. _Desperate Housewives_ or how much you adore those cute boys on _Entourage_. There is no shame in this addiction. If there is, I am in deep trouble.

Linda

If She Weren't Your Sister, Would She Be Your Friend?

Never praise a sister to a sister in the hope of your compliment ever reaching the proper ears.

Rudyard Kipling,
Plain Takes from the Hills, 1888

Compatibility Test

The foundation of a solid relationship, any relationship, is having mutual interests and hobbies, so you have to ask yourself: What do you and your sister have in common?

To find this out, examine the following list of things that women like to do and check off all activities that you enjoy sharing with your sister.

- ❑ Knitting
- ❑ Hiking
- ❑ Swimming
- ❑ Putting on a show
- ❑ Shoplifting
- ❑ Playing cards
- ❑ Spending your husbands' money
- ❑ Streetwalking
- ❑ Gossiping
- ❑ Rolling over and playing dead
- ❑ Running red lights
- ❑ Living in a fantasy world
- ❑ Brushing and flossing
- ❑ Bible class
- ❑ Punk rock concerts

❏ Dating inappropriate men (or women)
❏ Bragging about your children
❏ Contemplating suicide
❏ Getting manicures
❏ Exposing yourself in public
❏ Traveling
❏ Overeating
❏ Shopping
❏ Sacrificial rituals involving livestock
❏ Scouring toilets
❏ Reading
❏ Making a spectacle of yourself
❏ Going to therapy
❏ Triple XXX-rated flicks
❏ Giving, giving, giving till it hurts
❏ Feeling superior to other family members
❏ Reviewing personal wardrobe malfunctions
❏ Stalking ex-lovers
❏ Organizing charity events
❏ Throwing up after every meal
❏ Weeping uncontrollably for no apparent reason
❏ Failing to meet your parents' expectations
❏ Gardening

- ❑ Jumping to conclusions
- ❑ Quilting
- ❑ Drinking to excess
- ❑ Abusing postal workers
- ❑ Sewing
- ❑ Unnecessary surgical procedures
- ❑ Having anonymous sex with strangers in seedy hotel rooms
- ❑ Baking cookies
- ❑ Complaining about Mom
- ❑ Torturing small animals
- ❑ Making phony calls
- ❑ Never acting your age
- ❑ Hitchhiking
- ❑ Worshipping Satan
- ❑ Getting high
- ❑ Donating blood
- ❑ Group sex
- ❑ Shopping on eBay
- ❑ Arson
- ❑ Studying Torah
- ❑ Volunteer work
- ❑ Wallowing in self-pity
- ❑ Party planning

- ❏ Taking the Lord's name in vain
- ❏ Attending AA meetings
- ❏ Guitar lessons
- ❏ Practicing voodoo
- ❏ Ballroom dancing
- ❏ Living vicariously
- ❏ Downloading songs into your iPod
- ❏ Following the stock market
- ❏ Dressing in rubber

SCORE

To be friends: You will need to have at least twenty-five of these items in common.

To be sisters: You do not need to have any of these in common. She is your sister, whether or not you enjoy the same activities.

So, if you weren't related, would you be friends?

Improving Your Relationship with Your Sister

As we have shown in previous chapters, sibling relationships are among the strongest, most potent in human development. Yet there are no religious rituals that acknowledge sibling bonds, there are no national holidays celebrating "Sister's Day," no gift-giving occasions, and most important, no legal means to terminate the relationship. Much as you may try, you can never legally divorce your sister.

Consequently, you are stuck with this person for life.

Therefore, sisters need to know that their relationship can be stabilized. First, sisters should understand that within the family structure, siblings are a kind of subsystem: not as important as parent-child but slightly more meaningful than parent-pet with the possible exception of parents who own French poodles. Like most subsystems, though, the sibling relationship often breaks down and needs repairs that require great infusions of money, usually spent on a qualified therapist.

Sisters can improve their relationship by being more sensitive to each other's needs. To this end, here are suggestions and areas to consider in trying to become a better and more helpful sister. These suggestions cost me about $25,000 in shrink bills, but I offer them to you absolutely free of charge because, hey!, that's the kind of author I am.

Body Language

Communication between sisters breaks down into the following equation: 1 percent is verbal, 99 percent is nonverbal. In other words, *how* you talk to your sister is more meaningful than what you say to her.

Of course, you want to feel that, when you talk to your sister, you have her complete, undivided attention. How can you tell if your sister is really listening? Check for these telltale symptoms.

When you are revealing the most intimate details of your personal life to your sister:

1. Do her eyes wander all around the room?
2. Does she fidget and/or stare at her nails?
3. Does she make a phone call?

Once you have your sister's undivided attention, notice the messages being sent out by her body language. Gestures can convey a sister's true feelings. She could be saying something perfectly sweet and nice such as, "My, that's a lovely tattoo on your navel," but this comment is negated if, at the same time, your sister performs one of the following body motions:

1. Crosses her arms and raises her eyebrows
2. Crosses her eyes and bares her teeth
3. Holds up a cross and spits on the floor three times

Genuine Honesty

We all want to think that our sibling relationship is based on total honesty. On the other hand, most times sisters feel free enough to express their real feelings, and as any sibling knows, honesty can often be not only painful but also vicious as hell. For example, if you were feeling blue, how would your sister express her concern about you? Which questions would your sister be most likely to ask:

1. "Gee, is something bothering you?"
2. "Do you want to go somewhere and talk?"
3. "What the hell happened to you? Did you sleep in those clothes?"

If you were feeling self-conscious about a new outfit and wanted your sister's opinion, would you expect her to say:

1. "That color really flatters your skin tone!"
2. "Try a bright scarf around your neck. Here, I'll lend you my earrings."
3. "Have you gained weight recently? You look as big as a house."

Sisters should note the words they use with each other and remember that a small dose of honesty goes a very long way, especially in the 2000s. "I don't want my sister to be a phony," said the thirty-four-year-old waitress at my Greek restaurant, "but I wouldn't mind if she lied a little."

Exercises for a Better Sibling Relationship

Here's a question psychologists have long pondered: Why do we save keys long after we've lost (or moved away from) the locks to which they belong?

The answer is because keys symbolize solutions and solutions are hard to come by.

It's like life. As adults, we are left with a box full of assorted solutions even though we no longer know the problems to which they belong.

To sort out the complexities inherent in your relationship with your sister, try these helpful exercises and remember that this is not the time to indulge in the fantasy that your sister actually listens to your advice.

One: Imagine the perfect relationship between you and your sister.

How old are you?

Where do you live?

What is she doing to annoy you?

Two: Describe your sister as she would describe herself and have her do the same for you.

How closely do your descriptions match?

Are you on the same planet?

Three: If all else fails, tell your sister how much you love and appreciate her. Even if you are lying, it will make her happy and, who knows? someday you may actually mean it.

Tips and Advice

Being a sensitive and caring sibling is not just a sometime endeavor; it's a full-time job. To be done well, the job requires certain skills and a real effort on your part. You can do it by following these helpful suggestions:

1. Keep your expectations realistic. Your sister will never lend you that Prada dress she bought on sale, so quit asking.

2. Be descriptive, not judgmental, when discussing your sister's husband, lover, significant other, or live-in boyfriend. Sure, he's a creep and you don't understand what she sees in him. Be nice anyway. Offer him a beer. Smile politely. Laugh at his jokes. Thank your lucky stars you don't have to sleep with him.

3. Try to bring the power of positive thinking to your conversations with your sister. If, for example, you are walking with her on the beach in East Hampton or the Jersey shore and she sighs forlornly and says, "Oh, I am never going to be rich enough to own a house here," try to cheer her up. Tell her she has her health and her good looks. Do *not* remind her that she will never, ever be rich enough to even rent a house on any waterfront property anywhere in the world, with the possible exception of some parts of Louisiana.

4. If your sister starts to discuss something that really bothers her, reply by targeting the specific problem and not her entire personality. For example, if she

talks about financial difficulties, discuss the possibility of her asking for a raise or doing freelance work. This is called effective criticism. Do not say, "You're so insecure. When are you going to grow up? And it would be nice if you called Mom once in a while."

5. Be supportive when your sister's husband leaves her for his dental hygienist. Hold your sister's hand, cry with her, pat her back, and make her favorite macaroni and cheese recipe. Do *not* mention that you are currently lobbying for your married boyfriend to leave his wife. Your sister will never take kindly to such news. Trust me on this.

6. Avoid areas of conflict and subjects that are unsolvable, such as the way your sister drives a car, combs her hair, wears a short skirt, or feeds her children. Discuss topics upon which you can agree, such as the latest episode of *The Amazing Race* and/or the sex life of Tom Cruise and Katie Holmes. Agree to discuss only topics that have been featured in *People* magazine.

7. If your sister borrows your clothes and never returns them, remind yourself it is only because you have better taste and a more refined sense of style than she ever will. She can't help herself. All she really wants out of life is to look and dress like you, the poor thing.

8. When a woman marries, the expectation is that her sibling relationship will not change. This is totally unrealistic. Expect major upheavals and traumatic

confrontations, because nobody likes change and even fewer people like their brothers-in-law.

9. Never, ever criticize the way your sister disciplines her children. This is as dangerous as trying to come between Mama Grizzly Bear and her little cubs. The only time you are permitted to interfere is if you discover your nieces and nephews locked in the basement and they are begging for water. If they can convince you that they've been left alone for more than a week, then it is okay for you to hose them down. But first be sure to validate their timeline. You know how kids love to exaggerate!

10. When you and your sister disagree, the one who started the fight and cries the hardest gets her way, but she must also agree to have Mom over for the weekend. When all else fails, fight it out until one of you cries "Uncle." In the event of a tie, both sisters must go to their respective kitchens and neither is allowed to watch television for a week.

11. Schedule a pajama party for you and your sister every few months. Stay up late together and watch romantic comedies. Do each other's hair. Eat tons of chocolate and drink lots of cheap wine. Use this as a bonding time to heal and strengthen your relationship. If, however, you wake in the morning to discover that your sister has slipped off in the middle of the night to sleep with your husband, then you must insist that your next pajama party be held at her house.

12. Learn to listen. Adjust to your sister's style of communication, even if it means whining a lot. While she is talking, paraphrase her comments or say things like, "How interesting!" "How exciting!" or "Go on!" *Important tip:* Wait until her talking comes to a complete stop before offering your comments, advice, or constructive criticisms. While she speaks, don't sit on the edge of your chair, shaking your head frantically and waving your hand in the air trying to interrupt her. Do not fall asleep while she is talking, and never point a loaded gun at your sister unless you really intend to use it.

13. Take a night class together at your local college. If you can convince your sister to study automobile mechanics, you might save yourself a bundle on your next oil change.

14. Like any important task, the proper tools help get the job done right. So, too, it's imperative to use the proper tools for improving communication among sisters. These include:

    a. Kindness
    b. Support
    c. Tolerance
    d. Airplane tickets to Hawaii

15. Do not be annoyed when your sister e-mails off-color jokes to you several times a day. She will be insulted if you tell her to stop it. It only takes a moment to press "delete" and to remind yourself that, if your sister's

life were more interesting, she would have better things to do.

16. Avoid the labels of your childhood. Don't think of your sister as the Brain or the Pretty One or Miss Fancy Pants. You are no longer a child. It is time to grow up and treat each other like adults. So stick to the only labels that really matter: Dolce & Gabbana, Prada, and Tiffany, for example.

17. When shopping with your sister, never, never, never, ever suggest that she try on a larger size, especially if you drove to the mall in her car and need a ride home.

18. Offer to take your niece(s) and/or nephew(s) for an afternoon and give your sister some well-deserved alone time. Celebrate the kids' creativity and show them the kind of good time their mother doesn't understand. Take the kids to your local tattoo parlor and get them that gigantic skull and crossbones they've always wanted. Get your niece that pierced belly button ring and let the kids listen to the hard-core rap music that your sister will never appreciate. And don't forget how much kids love a massive sugar overload (almost as much as you do)! Since you have all that delicious disposable income, put it to good use on those kids. You don't have to be a child psychologist to know that a child's love can be bought.

19. The only appropriate responses when dealing with a jealous sister are indifference and pity. Indifference means never speaking badly of her and never speaking

to her at all unless absolutely necessary. Pity means keeping in mind that being jealous of someone is like swallowing poison and expecting the other person to die.

20. Admit that you were wrong about something. Confession is good for the soul and your sister will be so flabbergasted that she won't be able to talk for days. In such a state, she'll probably forgive you just about anything.

21. If you wake up one morning to discover that your life is perfect, that all of your dreams have come true, and that you are happier than you ever imagined you could be, then for heaven's sake, keep it to yourself! This is not the kind of information you should share with your sister. Not ever!

22. Finally, decide to stop treating each other as sisters and start treating each other as best friends. You may get her to lend you that Prada dress after all.

Epilogue:

Random Menopause Monologues

On the NPR quiz show *Whad'Ya You Know?* best-selling author Janet Evanovich was asked why she switched from writing romance novels to penning detective mysteries. She replied, "Well, I hit menopause and my thoughts suddenly turned to murder."

~

Ann Landers and Abigail Van Buren were known in newspaper syndication as *Dear Ann* and *Dear Abby*. For almost thirty years, Ann or Abby or both were named in the Gallup polls as the most admired women in America, in the *World Almanac* as among the most influential women in America, and in the *Ladies' Home Journal* among the one hundred most important women in America. Together, they were syndicated in over two thousand newspapers and reached an audience of more than two hundred million people.

Ann and Abby were identical twins, although plastic surgery greatly altered any semblance of their identical appearance from their childhood. Up until the age of twenty, they were inseparable. In fact, the first time they slept apart was on their wedding night. They were married in a double ceremony and honeymooned together as couples.

Were they close?

"There was never a time we weren't speaking to each other," Abby wrote.

"There were years when we weren't speaking," Ann wrote.

"I think being a twin is marvelous," Abby wrote.

"It isn't easy being a twin," Ann wrote.

"If these are twin sisters, I'll take cobras," said Mort Phillips, Abby's husband.

~

On May 3, 1988, the *New York Times* reported that a forty-member medical team successfully separated sixteen-month-old twin girls joined at the back of the head. The operation took place at a hospital on the outskirts of Johannesburg, South Africa.

The sisters' names were *Mpho*, which means "a gift," and *Mphonyana*, which means "less than a gift."

Appendix:

How I Researched This Book

This book will most certainly be hailed as a landmark work in the study of sibling relationships. At least my literary agent thinks so, as does my mother.

My aim in writing this book was to present the latest thinking, the most up-to-date research, any available psychological data, long-buried information, and historical perspectives, all combined with my own personal, highly biased, and subjective opinions. In short, I wanted to put together a groundbreaking, compellingly written volume that would sell like hotcakes.

In order to gather the latest thinking on the controversial subject of sibling relationships, I devoted long hours to the public library in downtown Los Angeles, which is conveniently located next to one of the best seafood restaurants in the city. However, since I find research incredibly boring, most of my time was spent writing long lists of things I wanted to buy with the advance money my publisher paid for the book, playing games on the new computers installed on the third floor, and eating clams on the half shell and Manhattan clam chowder at the outdoor tables next door. My intellectual stimulation came from trying to solve the daily crossword puzzle in the *L.A. Times* and deciphering a very complex wine list.

For lack of anything else to read, I began investigating my theories about sibling relationships by reading Nora Ephron, Delia Ephron, Hallie Ephron, and Amy Ephron and was encouraged to persuade my own sister to also write a book, or at least to start making lists. (She declined.) I read the Brontë sisters and their modern counterparts, the Collins girls. I went back to the romance comics of my youth. I reread *The Bad Seed*, which I once thought was based on my sister's life. Mostly though, I flipped through *People* for stories about the Hilton sisters and the Olson twins and prayed for lunchtime.

In addition to library research and reading, my information base was supplemented by extensive interviewing. Since I am basically a shy person and do not feel comfortable approaching strangers, I decided to limit my interviews to my close personal friends, asking everyone I knew embarrassing questions about their sisters.

Most of my friends and acquaintances were unwilling

to talk until I either revealed personal details of my relationship with my sister or intimate details of my sister's relationship with her husband, which she revealed to me in the strictest confidence. (Sorry, Sue, but this is for publication and I have a great many pages to fill.)

As a last resort, when all else failed to win over an unwilling subject, I used a tried and true journalistic tactic and offered cash.

In most cases, the cash worked best and I was able to garner enough material to make this book appear to cover a wide spectrum of different individuals. In truth, though, almost all my case studies come from people of the same social class, ethnic origin, life experience, and shoe size. We're all pretty much the same age, too—although I am a good six months younger than most of my friends, except for Janice C. who's still in her late twenties (but I don't hate her too much because she is at least thirty pounds overweight). I suppose I should add that almost every case history cited within this text is highly exaggerated.

I solicited diaries and letters from my case studies. I claimed I needed such data as additional pieces of evidence, but really, I wanted to read the stuff because I am just plain nosy and love to poke around in other people's personal belongings.

I followed leads whenever I could find them—which was almost never.

I taped all the conversations with my case studies so that I could quote accurately, but then unfortunately, I discovered I'd forgotten to put batteries in the tape recorder so I came away with almost nothing but blank tapes and lots of wasted energy spent punching buttons and carrying around additional batteries. (I'm no mechanical genius, that's for sure. It took me months to master TiVo.)

I tried to conduct most of my interviews in the subjects' homes so that I could make a firsthand evaluation of where and how they lived. Also, it saved me a bundle in restaurant bills. Most of the time, I got offered a cup of tea or a drink—if not an invitation to dinner—from my subjects. For this reason, I highly recommend this interviewing procedure to my fellow writers.

I preserved the anonymity of everyone who participated in my research so that no one would sue me after publication.

To expand the range of my raw data, I attempted to include repeated interviews over the course of several months with my subjects. However, as often happens among the best of friends (and certainly among sisters), I frequently fought with my subjects and stopped talking to them for extended periods of time. This made interviewing difficult, if not impossible. It was at this point in my research that I decided, as a way of saving energy for both myself and my subjects, to fabricate most of my case studies. This method proved to be a great time-saver, and because I did not have to schedule interview times, I got to watch my favorite daytime soap operas. In addition, with my imaginary data, I was able to prove every point I wanted to make.

I also made up quotes whenever it suited my purpose. My objective was not so much accuracy as completion.

I only had eight weeks to deliver a finished manuscript.

I discovered that once I gave up trying to be factual about every little point of reference, I was able to whiz through the manuscript in less than two weeks—although to my credit I should add that *twice* I worked past six o'clock. Once, I even worked on a Saturday night. (Top that, Miss Diane Sawyer, or, excuse me, should I say—Mrs. Mike Nichols.)

By finishing so quickly, I had a good six weeks to proofread and polish the final draft of my manuscript. Instead, I decided to shop at Fred Segal in Hollywood where—I'm thrilled to report—I spotted Lara Flynn Boyle trying on a skimpy silk halter and Tori Spelling eating a salad in the café.

I should add that, in case you're wondering, my qualifications for writing a book about sisters are many. First, I have a sister. Second, I once edited a book of sappy, sisterly love quotes called *No Friend Like a Sister*. And, finally, I am always pretty desperate for any amount of advance money. (I need not explain my financial difficulties to any single woman living above her means in the 2000s. I mean, the mortgage payments alone could break you, not to mention the cost of Ugg boots, not the knockoffs.)

As for my sister, I hope she will be a good sport about this book. If not, I'm telling.